KW-052-065

THE LOCAL ENVIRONMENT

Richard Kemp

Macdonald

GEOGRAPHY
10-14

A MACDONALD BOOK

© Macdonald & Co (Publishers) Ltd 1984

First published in Great Britain in
1984 by Macdonald & Co (Publishers) Ltd
London & Sydney

A member of BPCC plc

ISBN 0 356 09348 4

Printed and bound
by New Interlitho, Italy

Macdonald & Co (Publishers) Ltd
Maxwell House
74 Worship Street
London EC2A 2EN

Acknowledgements

The publisher would like to thank the following for
permission to reproduce photographs:

(Numbers refer to pages and T, B, R, L, indicate top, bottom,
right and left) 4 TL ZEFA, BL Alan Hutchinson, BR Spectrum
Colour Library; 5 TL Alan Hutchinson, TR J. Allan Cash Photo
Library, B Alan Hutchinson; 9 ZEFA; 13 Barnaby's Picture
Library; 14 B Greater London Council Photograph Library, T
Photo Nick Oates (Photon); 16 Spectrum; 19 Aerofilms; 20
Spectrum; 22 Original in the museum of the Public Record
Office, London (ref E31/2); 24 Topham; 26 Aerofilms; 27
BBC Hulton Picture Library; 28 Daily Telegraph Colour Lib-
rary; 29 J.S. Nettlefold, *Practical Housing*, London, 1910; 33
ZEFA; 35 TL Glass Manufacturers' Federation/Photo
Rosemary Weller, TR BPCC/Aldus Archive, B Clive Wood-
ley/Bruce Coleman Ltd; 36 T Spectrum Colour Library, B
Courtesy Marks and Spencer plc; 38 Topham; 39 Barnaby's
Picture Library; 40 T *The Graphic*, 1883, courtesy Norfolk
County Library, BL Courtesy of the City Engineer of Norwich,
BR Photo C.S. Middleton; 42 T The Architectural Press
Ltd/Stanley Travers, B The Architectural Press Ltd; 44 T
Farmer's Weekly Colour Library, B Mary Evans Picture
Library; 46 T Courtesy the Japan Information Centre, Lon-
don, B ZEFA.

Cover photograph:

Whitby Town and Harbour (FOTOBANK)

The illustrations are by Leon Baxter, for hand tinting print on
p.40; Robert Burns, pp. 9, 15, 18, 21, 27, 29, 41; Gary Hincks,
pp. 12, 21, 45, 47; Kevin Maddison, pp. 6-7, 8, 11, 15, 17, 36;
Raymond Turvey, pp. 10, 19, 23, 25, 31, 32-33, 34, 37, 43.

GEOGRAPHY 10-14

Series Editor: Richard Kemp,
Head of the Humanities Faculty,
Lord Williams's School, Thame

The Local Environment

Editor: Michèle Byam
Designer: Sally Boothroyd
Picture Research: Suzanne Williams
Production: Susan Mead

Series Consultants:
Barbara Hamnett, Head of the Geography Dept.,
JFS Comprehensive School, Camden, London
David Robinson, Headmaster, Blue Coat School, Dudley
Michael Storm, Staff Inspector of Geography, Inner London
Education Authority
Michael Weller, Co-ordinator PGCE Programme,
Bulmershe College of Higher Education, Reading
David Wright, Lecturer at the School of Education,
University of East Anglia, Norwich

Contents

Different Local Environments

The planet we all live on is in fact quite a small one. The Earth's mass is 330,000 times smaller than the sun, and there are stars in other galaxies far larger than our sun! To us though, the Earth is a large place: far too large for one person to possibly visit every place and corner in one lifetime. For most people the only part of the Earth's surface that they know well is the tiny piece around where they live. This is their **local environment**.

The word environment simply means 'surroundings'. You are probably reading this in the surroundings of your school — your school environment. Your school in turn is only one part of the local environment where you live. Your local environment will be partly **natural**, and partly **artificial**. The natural parts of the environment include the air you breathe and the soil — these are the pieces of the environment provided by nature. Much of your environment though will be artificial — in other words made by people. This is particularly true if you live in a large town or city. Even in farming areas most of the environment is made by people, as the original natural plants and trees will have been replaced or changed by farm crops and animals. In Britain today there are now very few truly natural environments.

Throughout the world people live in many different local environments. Just a few of them are shown in the photos.

Left: Figure 1. Below left: Figure 2. Below: Figure 3

Above left: Figure 4. Above right: Figure 5.
Right: Figure 6

1 Which of the photos shows a scene that is most like your local environment?

2 Which photos show scenes that are the most unlike your local environment? Write down why the places are so unlike your local area.

3 Each sentence below matches one of the photos. Which sentence matches which photo?

A Summer in an Eskimo village in Greenland
B An Indian village in a clearing in the Amazonian jungle
C A settlement in Tauranga, New Zealand
D Tents belonging to the nomadic Tuaregs of the Sahara Desert
E High-rise flats provide homes for many families in Hong Kong
F A floating home in Thailand

4 Write down what the word environment means.

5 What is the difference between the natural and artificial parts of an environment? Give some examples of both natural and artificial parts of your local environment.

6 You probably know your local area quite well. But how would your area look to someone from a very different part of the world? Write a description of your local area for someone who has never been there, and perhaps lives in one of the very different environments shown in the photos.

Look Around You – Your School

During the next few years you will be spending a lot of time at school. So how much do you know about your school?

– how many pupils are there?
– what age are the youngest and oldest pupils?
– how many teachers are there?
– when was the school first started?
– were all the buildings built at the same time?
– if not, when was the last building finished?

A school is quite a complicated organisation. Everyone in the school has to know where to go at what time – there would be chaos if there was no properly organised timetable! But a school is more than just a place where lessons happen. There are kitchens for cooking meals, a caretaker who organises the cleaning of the school, an office for all the administration that has to be done if the school is to run smoothly.

Let's start by looking at the part of the school you see most – the classroom. You probably have different lessons in rooms of different shapes and sizes.

1 Which room in the school do you spend most time in?

2 Which is the largest room you have lessons in?

3 Are there any rooms in the school that are always used for teaching the same subjects?

4 Fig. 1 is a **plan** of a typical classroom. As you can see it is a properly drawn plan – the size of the room has been measured by pacing, and all the things in the room have been marked on the plan.

Draw a proper plan of your own classroom. Here are some points to help you:

– first, make a rough plan of the room and the things in it.
– then take your measurements, and note them on your rough plan.
– draw your proper plan on squared paper, as this will help you to make things the correct size and shape. Use pencil at first, until you are sure the plan is right!
– finally, remember to give your plan a title to explain what it shows.

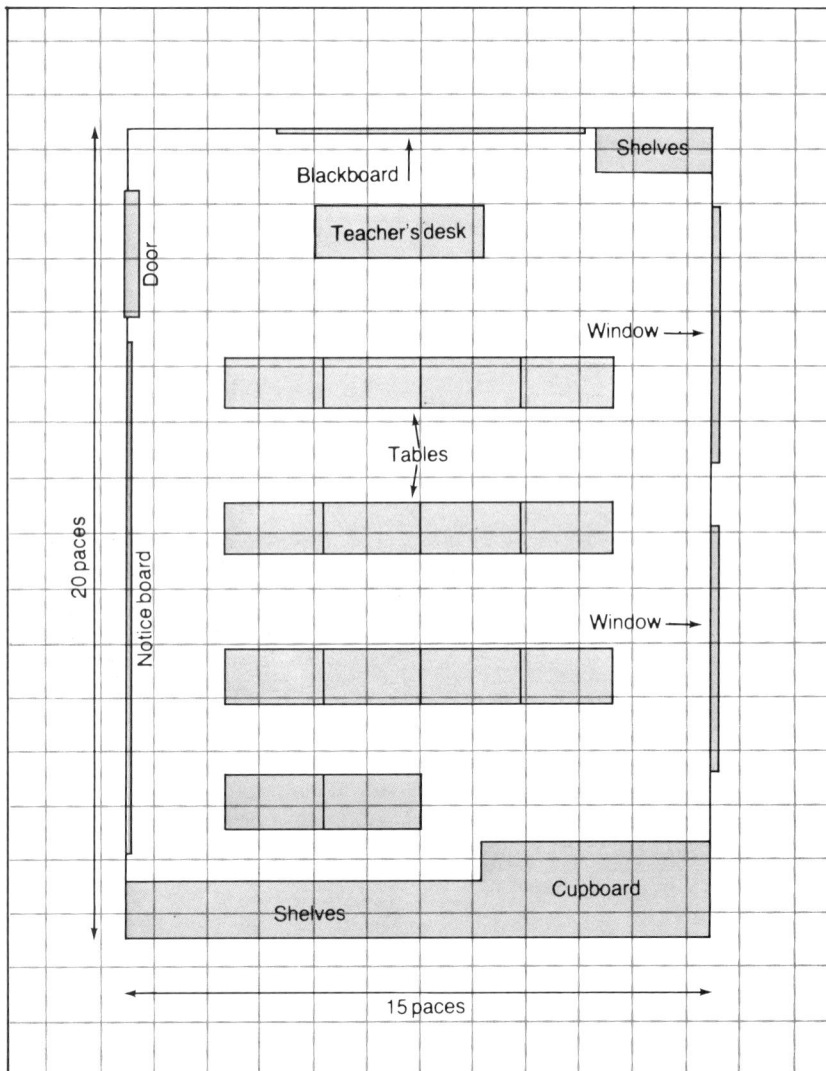

Figure 1

Each classroom is only a part of the larger environment of the whole school. A plan, or **map**, of the whole school would be more complicated than a classroom plan. Fig. 2 is a picture of a school. Fig. 3 is a map of the same school.

5 Look at the picture: how many buildings in the school are more than one storey high? How are these buildings shown on the school map?

6 By comparing the map and picture, say what each of the lettered places on the picture are used for.

7 For this question use *either* a neat copy of the school map shown in Fig. 3, *or* if you can, a map of your own school.

The school shown on this page has 750 pupils and teachers, or 30 classes of about 25 people. (If you are going to use a map of your own school remember that the numbers will probably be different.) At different times of day the people in the school are found in different places.

(a) On your plan show where people are likely to be found during normal lesson time. Using one colour, put one large dot for each group of about 25 people.
(b) Using dots of a second colour, show where the people would be found during school assembly.
(c) Using dots of a third colour, show where you think people might be found during the lunch hour.

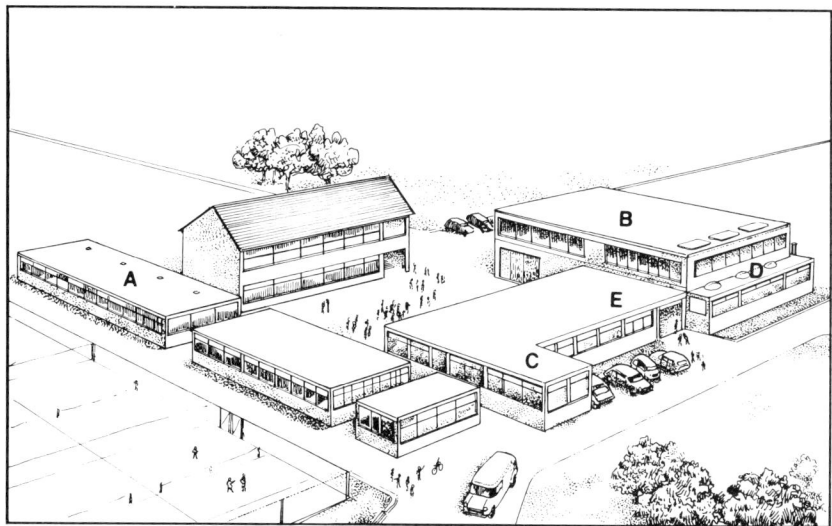
Figure 2

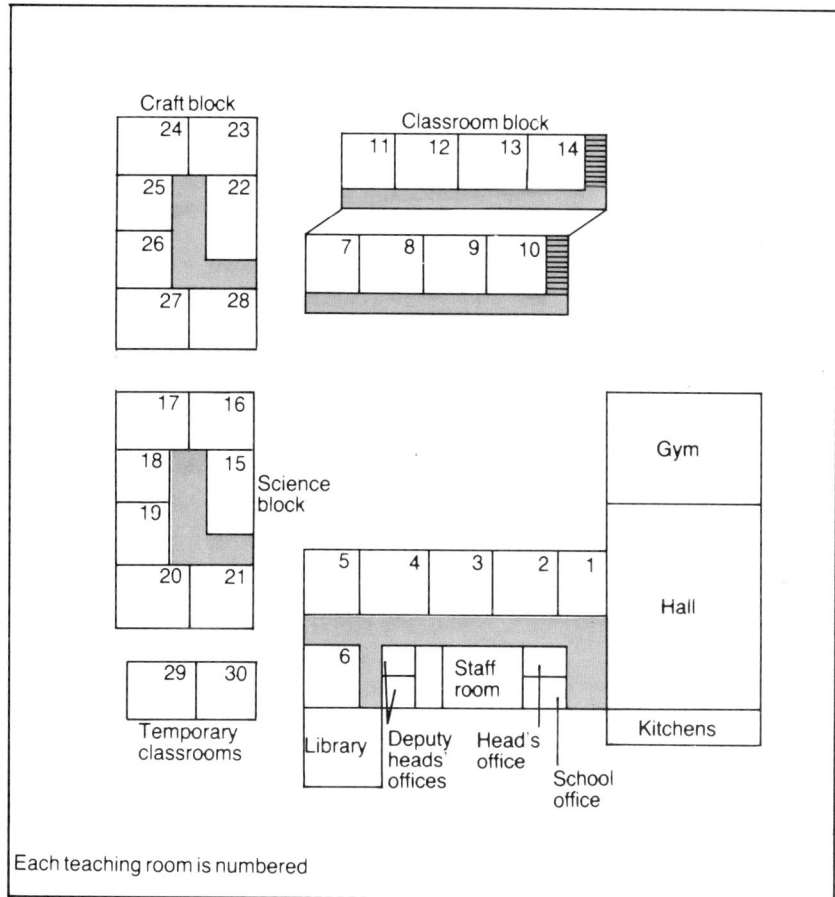
Figure 3

8 For someone who does not know their way around, a school can be a confusing place. Draw a simple sketch map of your school, which would explain to a visitor how to get from the school office to the room where you are now. Add the sort of labels that a visitor would find useful in finding their way around.

9 Write a description of your school for someone who has never seen it. Write about the size of the school, the type of buildings and how they are organised.

Moving About

What is the longest journey you have ever made? On their missions to the moon the American astronauts went on a return trip of 768,800 kilometres.

Occasionally you may go on quite a long journey, perhaps to go on holiday. But most of your journeys will be in your local area, to places near where you live.

Fig. 1 shows the movements of the Jones family during one day, and the box below tells you a little about the Jones's.

Mr Bob Jones

'I'm a sales representative, and so I have to travel around a lot. I've got a company car though. Even so I usually have a pretty long day.'

Mrs Sheila Jones

'Now that the children are a bit older I have gone back to work again for four mornings a week. It's very convenient, just a short bus ride.'

Peter Jones

'I left school last summer. I'm still looking for a full-time job. I do work down at the local garage though, for two or three afternoons a week, more if they are busy.'

Tracey Jones

'I'm still at school, in the third year. I usually go to school on my bike. I used to go home for lunch, but now that Mum is working I take sandwiches.'

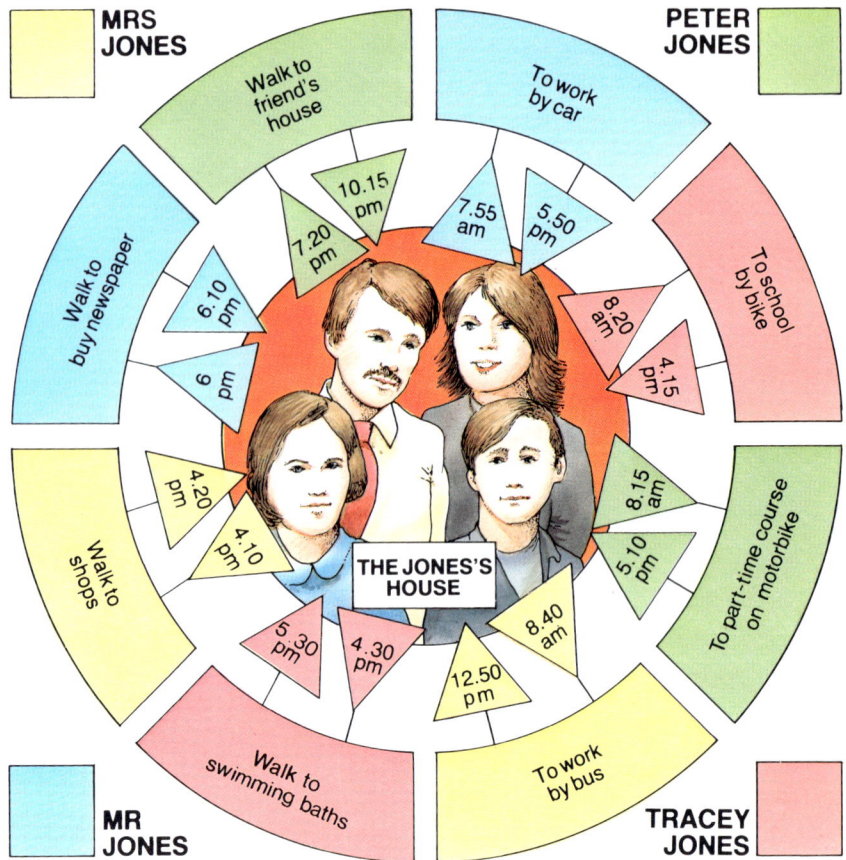

Figure 1

1 (a) How many different journeys did the family make during the day?
(b) Who was first out of the house in the morning?
(c) How many different types of transport were used?
(d) Who probably made the longest journey in that day?

2 Work out a timetable of the Jones family's movements during the day. List the movements in the order in which people left the house, using the table below as a guide.

3 Think back to your movements on a recent school day, and a recent weekend day.

Draw a diagram like Fig. 1 to show your movements on the two days – use a different colour for each day. (You may not remember the exact times of your movements, but that does not matter.)

Person Making the Journey	Time Left	Time Returned	Type of Transport
Mr Jones	7.55 a.m.	5.50 p.m.	Car
Tracey	8.20 a.m.	4.15 p.m.	Bike

The Jones family live in Northampton. Mr Jones is a sales representative. For his job he has to travel to many different places in the area around Northampton. Mr Jones tries to organise his week so that he does not have to drive too far in any one day.

The map (Fig. 2) shows the journeys he usually makes on Monday and Tuesday of each week. At the bottom of the map there is a **scale**. A scale is what we use to measure distances from a map. This type of scale is called a line (or linear) scale.

This line scale is marked off in intervals of 1 centimetre. It shows that every centimetre on the map represents 10 kilometres on the actual ground.

We can be more accurate than this. There are 10 millimetres in each centimetre. This means that each millimetre on the map represents 1 kilometre on the ground. Notice that this is written by the scale – this is called a statement of scale.

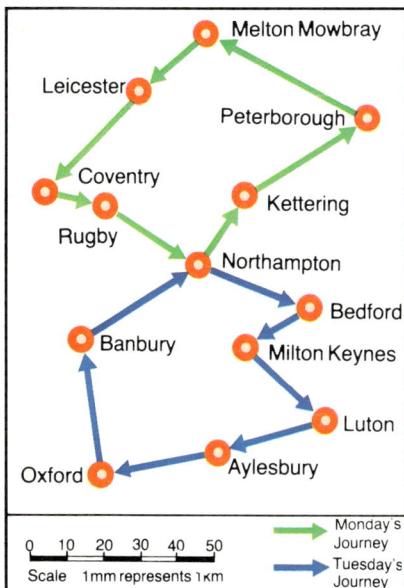
Much of Mr Jones's working day is spent on the road

4 Make a copy of the table below (Fig. 3). Use your ruler to work out the distances between Northampton and the places shown. Write your measurements in the spaces on the table.

From Northampton	Map Distance in mm	Ground Distance in km
To Bedford		
To Luton		
To Oxford		
To Coventry		

Figure 3

5 The green line shows Mr Jones's Monday journey. The arrows show the route he takes. Work out the total distance he drives – draw a table like Fig. 4, and fill in the names of the places he visits, and the distances between them.

6 How far does he drive on Tuesday? Draw a second table to work this out.

7 On which day does he have the furthest to drive?

8 In fact Mr Jones probably covers a greater distance than you have worked out. Why do you think this is?

9 Draw your own line scales to show these different map scales:
1 cm represents 20 km
2 cm represent 1 km
1 cm represents 5 km
1 cm represents 100 m

Monday's Journey	
Northampton to Kettering	22 km
Kettering to Peterborough	km
	km
	km
	km
	km
	km
Total Distance covered on Monday	km

Figure 4

Figure 2

Your Local Community

How many people do you meet in a day? In a normal school day it must be dozens. Fortunately, few people live such isolated lives that they have little or no contact with other people. Most of us live in a **community**. The people in your local area, your neighbours, friends and even people you don't know, form your local community.

We can only live the way we do because other people provide us with goods and services. Fig. 1 only shows the services that are provided for us at our homes. We depend on many other services as well, many of them provided by people in the local community.

Any community has a mixture of people – some retired, some working, some unemployed, some at school. Some people will have lived in the area for many years, others will be newcomers. Some people will live as families, others will live alone or with friends. No two communities will be exactly the same, because the mixture of people will always be different.

On the opposite page four people tell you a little about themselves and their local communities.

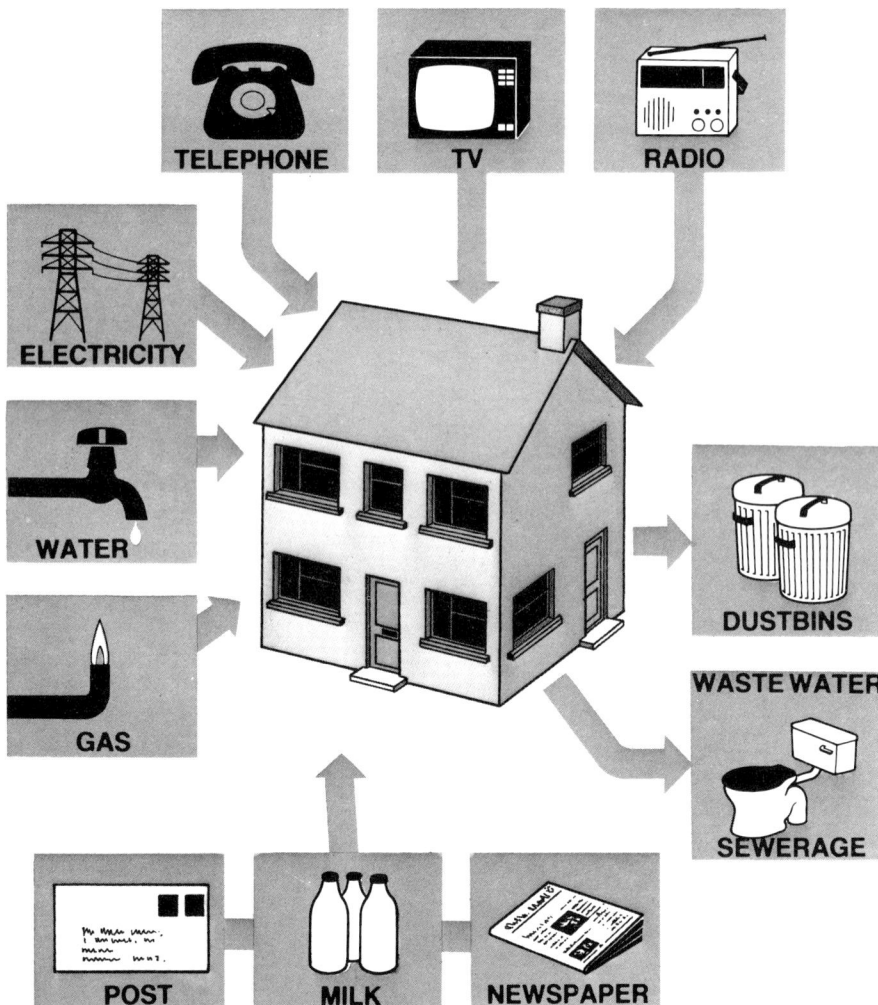

1 (a) Using Fig. 1 to help you, make a list of all the services provided for you at your home.
(b) For each service say who provides it for you.
(c) How many of the services on your list are provided by your local community?

2 What other local services do you and your family make use of?

3 Which of the four communities described on the opposite page is most like the one you live in?

4 Each of the four people think that there are some good and some bad points about living where they do. Take each one in turn, and list what they think are the *advantages* and *disadvantages* of living where they do.

5 Which of the four people live in communities where the majority of people know each other? Why do you think this is?

6 Describe the street and building where you live, and say how long you have lived there.

7 Make a list of what you think are the good and bad points about living where you do.

TELEPHONE
TV
RADIO
ELECTRICITY
WATER
GAS
DUSTBINS
WASTE WATER
SEWERAGE
POST
MILK
NEWSPAPER

Figure 1

Alec and Jean Washington live in a council house in a small village.

'We've lived here all our lives and in this house for the last 25 years. We know just about everyone in the village. I wouldn't want to live in a town – there's too much noise and rushing about. But many of the young people are leaving as there aren't enough jobs. We used to have a shop, but now there's only the pub. There aren't so many buses either. We've got a car, but not everyone has.'

Andrew Davis shares a flat in a house near the centre of the city.

'I moved here 2 years ago after I left university. My family live about 20 miles away and I sometimes go home for weekends. So far I've had difficulty in getting a permanant job as unemployment in this part of the country is really high. Still, there's lots going on here and I've made several friends. Most of the houses in this street need doing up and it's very noisy living on a main road. But public transport is good and there's a street market just round the corner.'

Mary Simpson lives in a high-rise flat in the city.

'I've lived in this city for 23 years, but I only moved into this flat 4 years ago. The house where I used to live was demolished. I have a proper bathroom now and a lovely view; still there's an awful lot of stairs if the lift isn't working! In my old street I knew everybody but I don't know many people here. But my daughter lives close by, and so I do see her more often.'

Anne Young and her family live in a semi-detached house on an estate.

'We moved here only last year. This estate is all right, it's not too big, and the houses are really modern. The kid's school is just round the corner, which is convenient. The main problem is that you've got to travel a couple of miles into town to do any shopping. You need a car to live here and I don't have the car during the day. Still, we do live near beautiful countryside.'

Past and Present

Just over 2000 years ago the Romans, under the command of Julius Caesar, invaded Britain. The country the Romans would have seen was very different from the Britain any tourist would see today.

When the Romans invaded there were less than half a million people living in Britain – today the population is over 100 times larger.

But at that time people occupied only a small part of Britain – today there are few places where people are not living and working.

The four drawings (Fig. 1) show how one area has changed since Roman times.

The story of how Britain has changed can be seen in almost every village, town and city. Any old building tells us something about what that place was like in the past. The most exciting examples are probably the ruined castles and abbeys left over from the Middle Ages. Old barns, farmhouses and mills tell us what life would have been like in country areas before people had modern machines and power. From more recent times there have been factories and houses built during the Industrial Revolution about 150 years ago. The great factories, with their tall chimneys, tell us something of what it must have been like to live and work in the new towns of the Industrial Revolution.

2000 YEARS AGO

500 YEARS AGO

100 YEARS AGO

TODAY

Figure 1

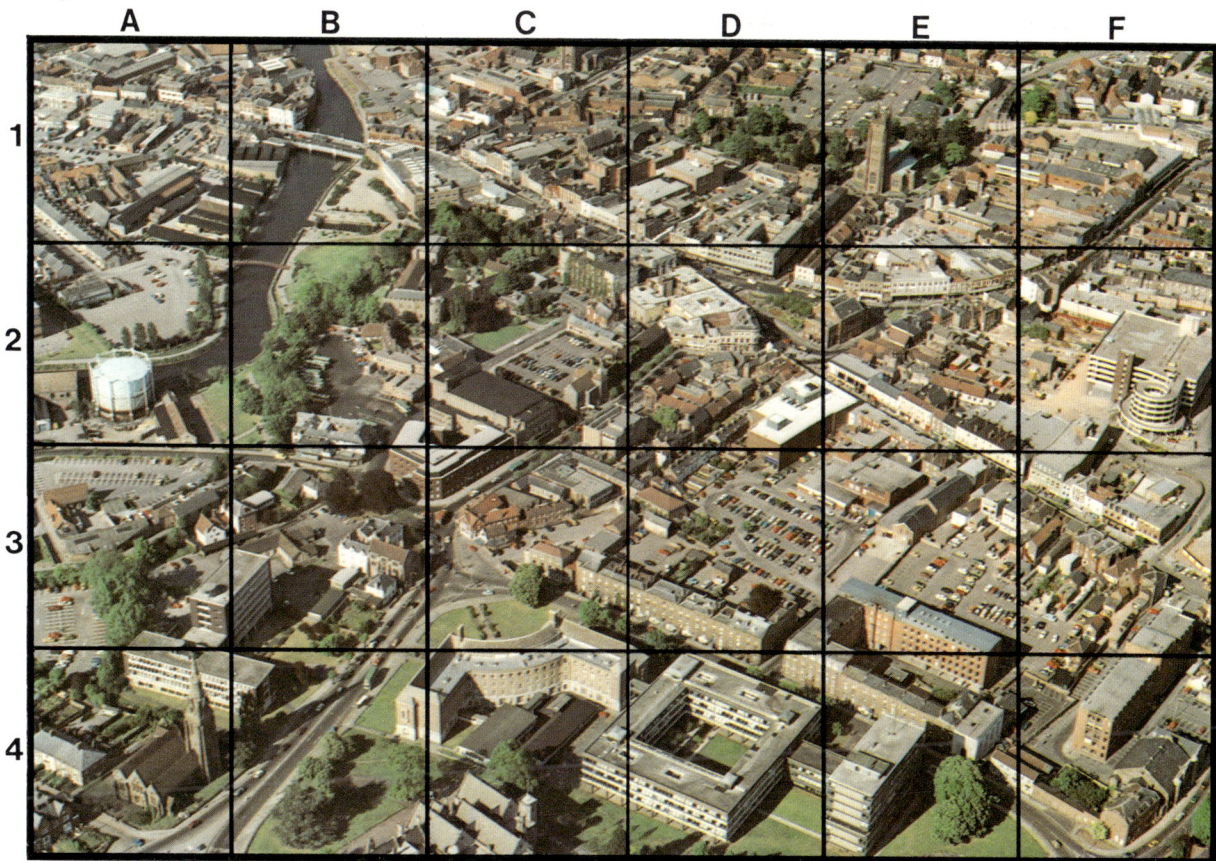

Aerial photograph of Taunton, Somerset

1 The bar graph (Fig. 2) shows how many people were living in Britain at different times since 1500.
(a) Work out Britain's population at each of the dates.
(b) During which 100 year period was there the biggest increase in the number of people?

2 Look carefully at the 4 drawings in Fig. 1:
(a) In your own words say what the area looked like 2000 years ago.
(b) In what ways did the area change between 2000 and 500 years ago?
(c) Describe how the area has changed between 500 years ago and today.

3 What two types of transport have only become important in the last 150 years?

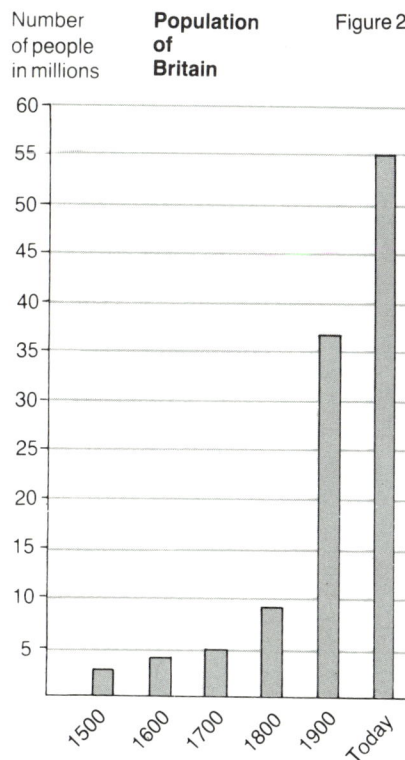

Number of people in millions

Population of Britain

Figure 2

4 Look at the aerial photo of Taunton, Somerset:
(a) How many churches can you see? Note down the squares in which they are found.
(b) Do you think that the large building in square D4 is old or new? Give the reasons for your answer.
(c) Pick out squares where each of the following are found: *car park* and *multi-storey car park, gasometer, bridges, office block, shopping street, rows of terraced housing*.

5 Name some old buildings in your local area. If you can, say what they were used for when they were built, and what they are used for today.
Do you know when they were built? If not, try and find out.

13

The Motor Age

The photo below is a view of an ordinary town street, on an ordinary day. There is nothing special going on, just the normal bustle of the town.

The photo underneath that is a view of that same street in 1912. Again there is just the normal bustle of the town – but with an important difference.

Today we live in the motor age. At the beginning of the century only the rich could afford cars. The cheapest car would have cost more than most people earned in a whole year. Then, in the 1920s, in America, Henry Ford developed a way to mass produce cars much more cheaply. He used the sort of assembly line methods still in operation today. Since then, although car prices have increased, they have not increased as fast as peoples' wages. Now more people than ever before own cars. Every year there are more lorries, buses, cars and motorbikes on the road. During this century our villages, towns and cities have changed faster than ever before. An important reason for this has been the coming of the car. Today we take for granted things like traffic lights, road signs, bus stops, and the noise and smell of traffic – at the beginning of the century they simply did not exist. The coming of the car is an important reason, though not the only one, which explains why the pace of life is now much faster than it was 100 years ago.

Swiss Cottage, North London in 1983 (top photo), and 1912

1 Towns today have to cope with a lot more road traffic. Look carefully at the two photos – list any of the things to do with road traffic that are there today, but were not there 70 years earlier.

2 How many building changes can you see? Make a list and say what the change is in each case.

3 Fig. 1 shows how the number of cars on Britain's roads has increased over the last 50 years. Draw a bar graph to show this information.

4 Why do you think that more people than ever before own cars?

5 The fact that more people own cars has brought not only advantages, but disadvantages as well. What do you think are the advantages and disadvantages?

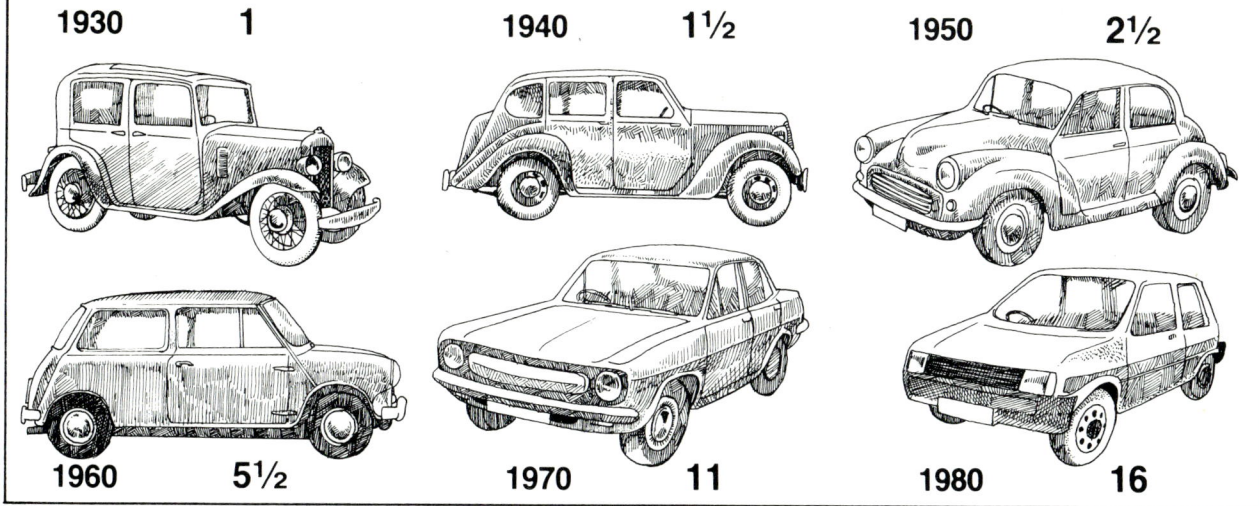

Number of cars in Britain – in millions

| 1930 | **1** | 1940 | **1½** | 1950 | **2½** |

| 1960 | **5½** | 1970 | **11** | 1980 | **16** |

Figure 1

Survey Idea

In any town or city there have to be ways of controlling traffic – where cars can go, where they can park, and so on.

Aim – what is the survey for?
To find out the different ways traffic is controlled.

Location – where is the survey to be carried out?
A busy shopping street in your local area.

Method – how is the survey to be done?

You are going to walk along the street you have chosen, and note down all the ways that are used to control traffic.

1 Decide exactly which part of the street is to be surveyed. At the top of a sheet of paper put the name of the street, the place where the survey is to start, and a note of the time and date of the survey.

2 Draw 2 lines across your paper this represents the street. As you walk along note anything, either on the road or by the road, which helps to control traffic. The diagram below (Fig. 2) gives you some ideas on how to do this.

3 On your return use colours to make a good copy of the information you collected.

Results – what did the survey show?

How many different ways of controlling traffic did you find?

What were they?

Was this more or less than you expected?

Do you think that there are any ways the control of traffic in that area could be improved?

Figure 2

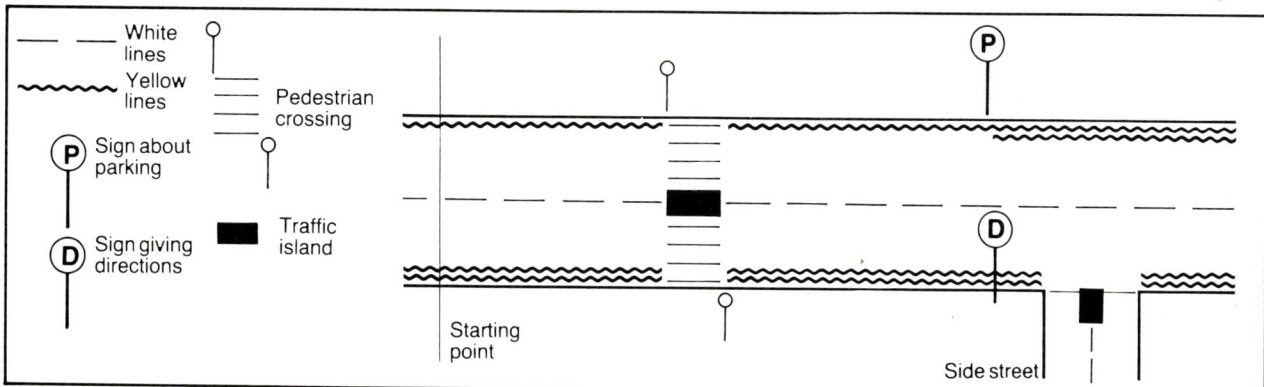

15

How Have Buildings Changed?

Any large company that makes bricks, or tiles, or windows, or any other building materials, expects to sell its products throughout Britain. Modern methods of road and rail transport mean that building materials can be taken anywhere in the country. Modern methods of production mean that materials made in one place are very like the materials made somewhere else. The result is that a new house in one place may look very like other new houses all over Britain. No area has its own special style of building.

A few centuries ago things were very different. There was no easy way of moving building materials. Wherever possible people used local materials to build their houses. Where there was stone available, they built houses of stone with stone slate roofs. Where there was no stone they built houses with thatched or tiled roofs, and walls of timber and plaster, or brick.

The drawings on the opposite page show just some of the changes in building materials over the years. The drawings also show some of the changes in **building styles** – whatever the materials used, old buildings look very different from new ones.

1 Using page 17, describe how the size and shape of windows has changed over the years.

2 Make a list of the different building materials used for old buildings. Are any of these materials used for old buildings in your area?

3 In your own words explain why old buildings in different areas look so different, while new buildings often look very much the same.

4 (a) In which period was your home built?
(b) Make a drawing of your home, and describe the building materials of which it is made.

5 Why is it that only very new houses:
(a) do not have chimneys?
(b) do have built-in garages?

6 The photo (Fig. 1) shows a building that has had parts added to it at different times.
(a) Which do you think are the oldest and newest parts of the building?
(b) How many different parts seem to have been added on to the building? In what age periods do you think they were built?

7 **Project idea:** Choose 3 very different buildings in your local area. Do a careful drawing of each. On your drawing say what building materials were used. Try and say which age period the building belongs to.

8 **Project idea:** Find out about the oldest buildings in your local area. When were they built? Who built them? What were they used for?

Figure 1: Balliol College, Oxford

OLD – Before 1800

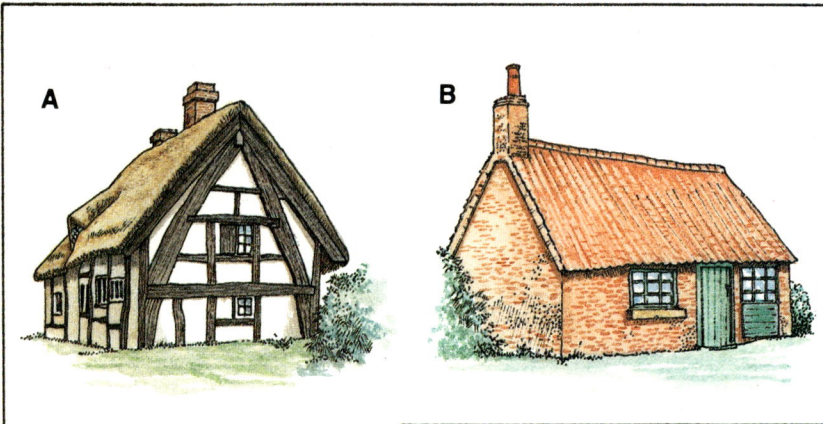

A Roof – thatch
Walls – timber and plaster

B Roof – red tiles
Walls – old brick

C Georgian brick town house

Old houses are made of many different materials. They are also of many different shapes and sizes. By the 1700s many houses were becoming more regular in shape and design – this is called the Georgian period.

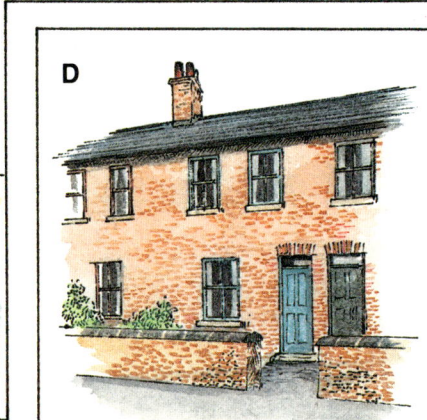

VICTORIAN 1820 – 1920

D 2-bedroom terrace house
Roof – blue slate
Walls – brick

E Large town house
Roof – blue slate
Walls – brick and plaster

In the 1800s towns grew rapidly. Rows of terraced houses were built to house the people who worked in the new factories. Large town houses were built for wealthier people.

NEW – Since 1920

F Semi-detached house
Roof – tiles
Walls – brick

G Modern House
Roof – tiles
Walls – brick

H Modern block of flats
Material – concrete blocks

Between 1920 and 1950 many semi-detached houses were built near the edge of towns. Since 1950 many houses have been built on estates.

Planning for Change

Whether it is in the town or country, we all want to live in pleasant surroundings. Not long ago, if you owned a plot of land, you could build almost anything you liked on it. But by the 1930s people began to realise that it was not a good thing to have no control over what was being built. For one thing, other people might be badly affected by what was being built, or a beautiful part of the environment might be spoiled.

A number of **Acts of Parliament** have now been passed making local councils responsible for the proper planning of new buildings and other developments in their area. Before any new building can be put up, whether it is a house, warehouse, factory or whatever, the builder has to draw up proper plans and give them to the local council. The council then decides whether or not to give **planning permission**.

Before giving planning permission, a council might ask the following questions about the new building or development:

Would people already living in the area be seriously affected by the new development?

Would the local environment be seriously damaged?

Would the road access be good enough, or might the development be a danger to people or traffic?

Is it the right sort of development for that particular place in the local area?

It was in the cities that proper planning control was most needed. As the cities grew larger, more and more farmland and open space surrounding the cities was swallowed up by new buildings. Every new house or factory at the edge of the city means that, for the people living in the city, the open countryside is a little bit further away.

The first city to draw up a proper plan to control its growth was London in 1947. The planners made a **Green Belt** around London, as Fig. 1 shows. In the Green Belt there is very strict control over new building, and so a ring of farmland and open space is protected from any further growth of the city. As Fig. 2 shows, other cities have since followed London's example.

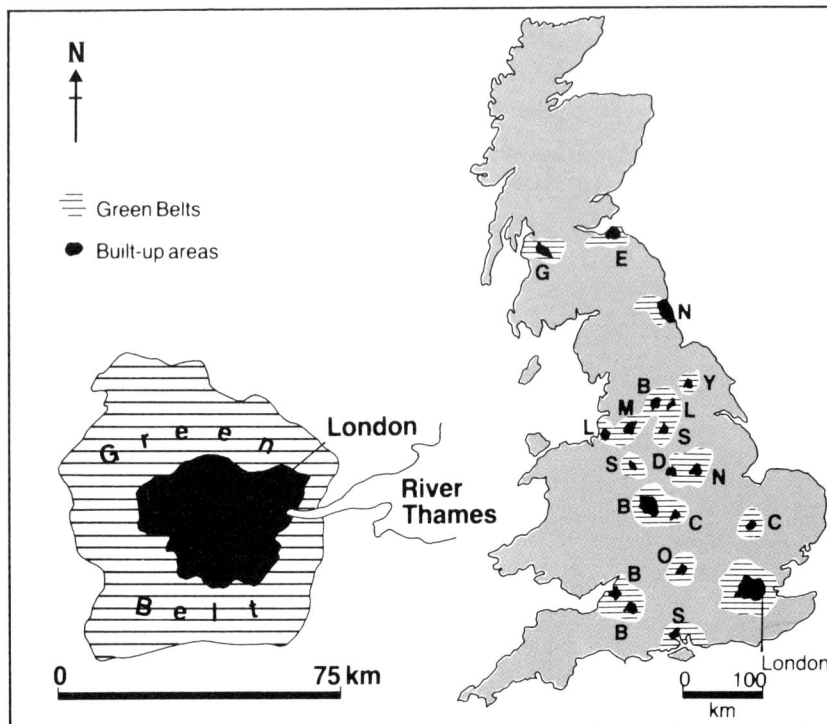

1 In your own words explain what a Green Belt is, and what it is for.

2 How many major cities in Britain are completely or partly surrounded by Green Belts?

3 Use your atlas to name the Green Belt cities shown by their initials on Fig. 2.

4 Some new buildings have to be built in the Green Belt areas, because the people live and work there, and cannot move elsewhere. Try and think of some examples.

Figures 1 (left) and 2 (right): The Green Belt around London and other British cities

Planning Study

Fig. 3 shows the plans of a new warehouse that a company, GC Supplies Ltd, would like to build. The company would use the warehouse to store building materials, which would then be sent out by lorry to a number of construction sites in the local area.

Study the plans carefully, and then answer these questions:

1 Describe what the warehouse would look like – say what size it would be, and what sort of materials would be used to build it.

2 How does the company want to use the warehouse?

3 How would vehicles get to and from the warehouse?

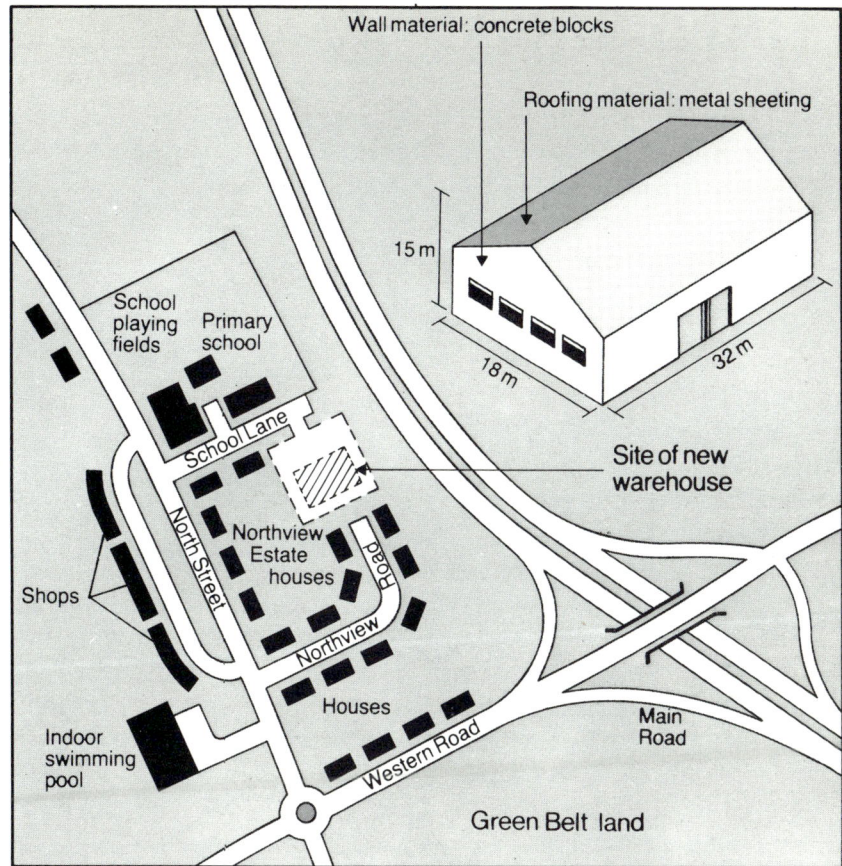

Figure 3

4 What other buildings surround the site where the warehouse would be?

5 What possible advantages and disadvantages might the new warehouse bring to people already living in the area?

6 If you were the local council would you give planning permission for the warehouse to be built? Say either 'Yes' or 'No', and then give reasons for your decisions.

7 Why would the council certainly not give permission for the warehouse to be built in the open land on the other side of the main road?

Green Belt area around Southampton

Why Build There?

Ask a group of people 'where would you most like to live?', and you would probably receive a variety of answers (see below).

Some people are quite happy living where they do. Other peoples' idea of an 'ideal' place may be miles away from where they are living now. It is not surprising that different people would choose very different places, because the reasons for their choices will vary from person to person.

Hundreds of years ago groups of people chose where to settle in Britain for other reasons. In those days there were far fewer people living in this country, and there were hardly any towns and villages. Large parts of Britain were almost empty. The early

Scarborough, Yorkshire, had an easily defended site on the coast

settlers came from various parts of Europe. Most of them were farmers, and their reason for coming to Britain was to find good land to farm.

Life for the early settlers was hard. They were on their own. To survive they simply had to produce enough food for

themselves. Because of this their choice of where to live was very important indeed. They had to choose a good place for farming.

What things did they have to think about when choosing a place to live and farm? Some important points are listed in the box below.

'I like it here in town. We're close to the shops and schools. It's very convenient.'

My dream house would be a cottage in the country – somewhere quiet and peaceful.

'I don't have much choice, do I? I live here because it's close to my job.'

It's too quiet here, there's nothing to do. I'd like to live in a city, it would be much more interesting.

'I'd like to live somewhere warm! On a South Sea island – you know, blue seas, sunshine, and all that.'

An early farmer's choice of settlement site would be influenced by these locational factors:	
1	Is there a good supply of water close by? Water was needed everyday for drinking, cooking and washing.
2	Is there a supply of wood nearby? Wood was very important for building houses and tools, and for firewood.
3	Is the land good for growing crops and grazing animals? Is the land flat enough? Is there enough land clear of trees? Is the soil fertile?
4	Is the land likely to be flooded? Low lying land near rivers might flood, and this would be a serious problem.
5	Can the place be protected easily if it was attacked by other people?

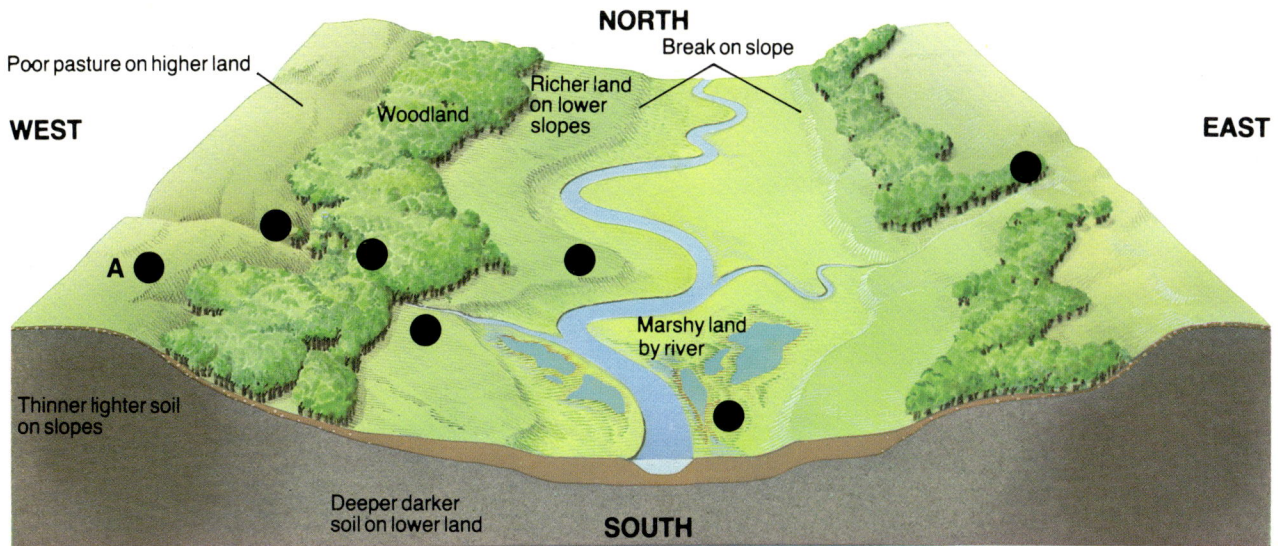

Figure 1

Imagine that you were one of the early settlers, and that you were moving into the area shown in Fig. 1. You have to choose a good place to set up your house and farm. Some possible sites are marked – which one would you choose?

1 Taking each site in turn:
(a) first write a sentence describing its position. For example, site A is 'on the higher land to the west of the river, above the woodland'.
(b) Then say how good the site is for all of the 5 points listed in the box on page 20.

2 After you have looked carefully at all the sites, make your final choice. Write down why you have chosen that place and not one of the others.

3 A map of the area around your farm would be very useful.
(a) Make a copy of the map grid (Fig. 2), and shade your farm in red.
(b) Using Fig. 1 mark the woodland and other features of the area onto your map.

4 What is the letter and number of the squares which have
(a) your farm site
(b) the two points where streams join the main river.

5 Use your atlas to trace a map of northwest Europe. On your map show the movement of these early settlers to Britain:

Romans – from Italy and France
Saxons – from Germany
Angles – from Germany
Vikings – from Norway
Danes – from Denmark

6 Write an account of the life of a farming family during their first year after settling in an unoccupied part of early Britain.

7 Imagine that you are living at the place you chose in Q2. You hear that a small band of men are attacking and burning farms. They seem to be moving towards your area. What would you and your family do?

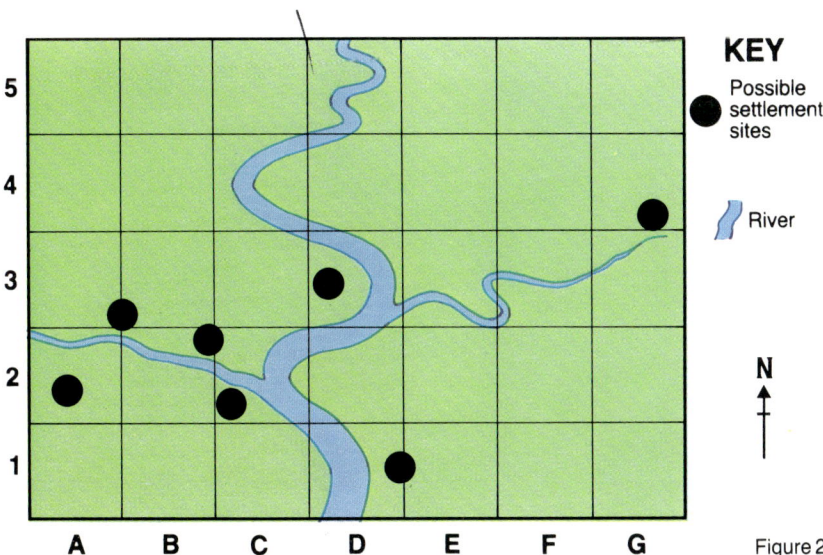

KEY

● Possible settlement sites

〰 River

N

Figure 2

What's in a Name?

What do the words Mousehole, Muck, Worminghall, Looe and Dumpdon all have in common? The answer is that they are all the names of places in Britain. There is an enormous variety of place names in Britain, and to find out why, we need to go back in time.

The chances are that the place where you live has a history that goes back at least 500 years, and probably for a thousand or more. Take Birmingham for example – today Birmingham is Britain's second largest city, but it started out as a tiny farming village almost 1500 years ago. Like most places its name has changed over the years. At first it was Beornmundingaham. In 1086 it was recorded as Bermingeham, and this has since changed to today's Birmingham.

One reason why there is so much variety in Britain's place names is because, in a way, we are all immigrants. For over 2000 years different peoples, speaking different languages, have been coming to settle in Britain. First to come were the Celts, then the Romans, and later the Angles and Saxons, and the Vikings and Danes. It was these early settlers who left the greatest mark on place names.

Most of them were farming people, and the names they used for their farms and villages were often to do with the land. The boxes give examples of common place name endings that were used by different groups of early settlers. The map (Fig. 1) shows where certain types of names are most common, and explains why.

The Domesday Book

A later group of settlers were the Normans, who came from northern France. They invaded England in 1066, and their leader, William the Conqueror, became king. One reason why we know so much about old place names is due to William. He ordered a full survey of the whole of England. The name and size of every settlement was recorded, even how much land each village farmed and how many animals were kept! William's purpose was to record exactly how much people owned, so that he could collect as much tax as possible. The survey was complete by 1086, and was written down in the Domesday Book – which we still have (see below).

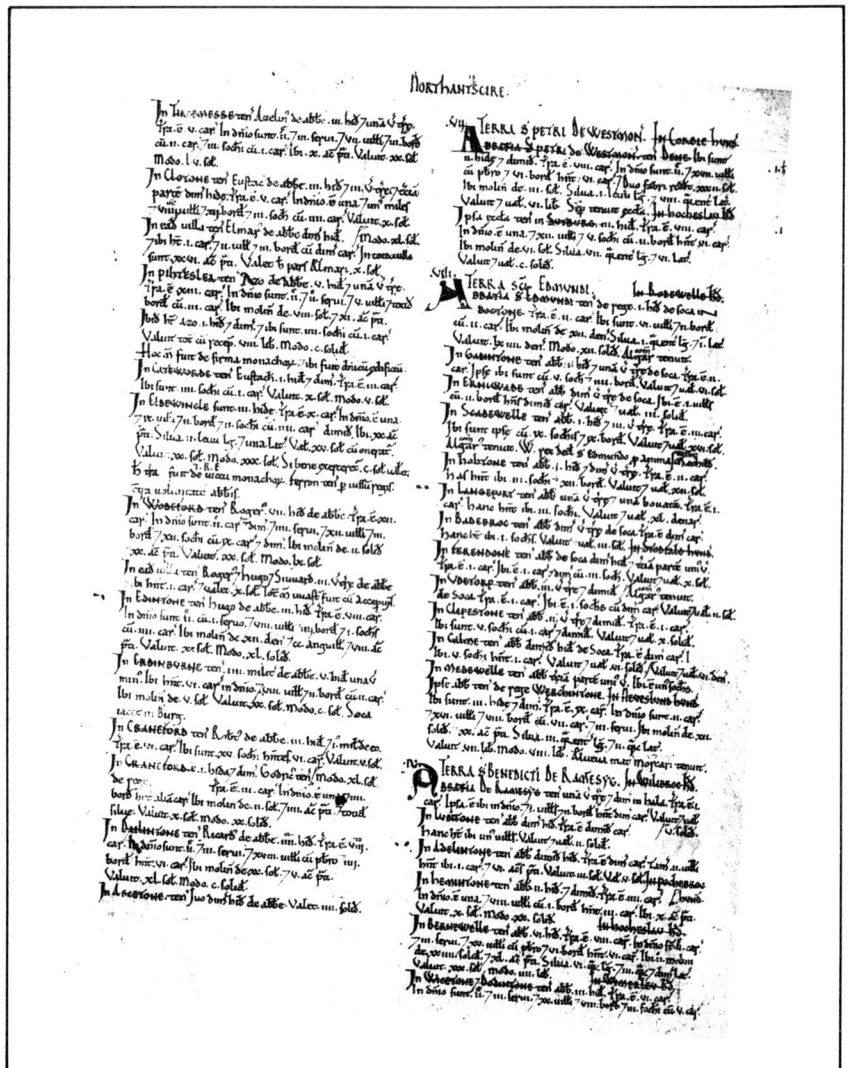

The Domesday Book. This page is the entry for part of Northamptonshire. It is written in Norman French, and so you will have difficulty in reading it!

Celtic names

The Celtic languages were Welsh, Cornish and Gaelic.

-aber = mouth of river
-avon = water
tre- = settlement
loch- = lake

Many of the place names that are difficult to pronounce are Celtic. Britain's longest place name is Welsh – Llanfairpwllgwyngyllgogerychwyrndrobwllllantysiliogogogoch. Try and say it!

Roman names

The Romans were a military people. They built many fortified camps. In their language, latin, the word for camp was *castra*. Over the years this changed to -caster -cester -chester. Manchester is one example.

Anglo-Saxon names

-ton, -tun, -on = farm
-ham = farm or homestead
-ing = settlement
-stead = place or building
-worth = field
-wick, -wich = farm
-ley, -leigh = clearing

Birmingham, for example, means the 'farm of Beormund's people'.

Scandinavian names

-thorpe = hamlet
-by = homestead or village
-thwaite = clearing

Whitby, for example, means the 'white village', probably from the colour of its buildings.

There are many other English name endings as well, for example
-bridge -ford -field -wood.

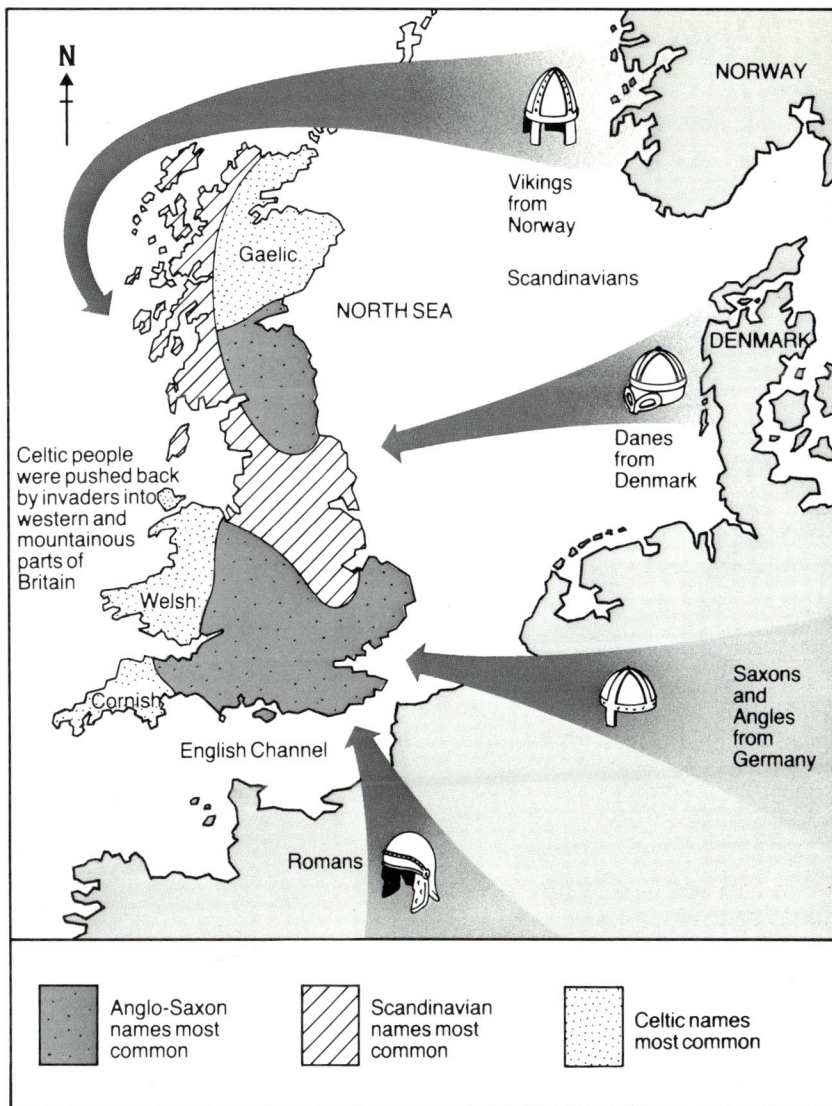

Figure 1

1 Make a list of all the name endings in the boxes. Then use your atlas to find at least one place as an example of each name ending.

2 Most early name endings meant something to do with the land. Why was this?

3 At one time the Celtic people lived all over Britain. Why are Celtic names now common in only a few parts of the country?

4 As well as the name endings you have listed, there are lots of other words commonly found in place names in Britain – *port* for example. Use your atlas to see how many you can find.

5 Use your atlas to try and identify towns and cities built by the Romans.

6 Do you know how the places in your local area got their names? Try and find out.

Market Towns

Have you ever wondered what Britain would have been like 500 or 1000 years ago? Certainly very different from today. For one thing you would not have understood the way English was spoken – it sounded very different then!

In those days most people lived in small farming villages. There were no hard surface roads, and the only way of getting about was on foot or horseback. Goods had to be moved by cart. This meant that people did not travel much. Many people lived all their lives in one village, and never travelled more than a dozen miles from it. In each village the people grew their own food, and made for themselves most of the other things they needed.

What they could not produce themselves they had to get from other people in the local area. So people needed to meet and trade. This trading happened at local **markets**. At regular times in the year people would meet at the market to buy and sell things. They met at a place where everyone could get to most easily – in other words the most accessible place in the local area. This is how **market towns** grew up.

The photo below shows a street market at Ormskirk in about the year 1880. It is a scene not very different from the markets of two or three hundred years earlier. Since 1900 things have changed though – the coming of the car has seen to that. Market towns today are still important local shopping and business centres, but many have grown much larger. They have more houses and schools, and often modern industries as well. Yet despite all the changes, many still have their weekly street markets.

A street market in Ormskirk, Lancashire, in about 1880

1 Look at Fig. 1. Explain why Overton grew into the local market town.

2 What does it mean to say that a place is 'accessible'?

3 Look at the map (Fig. 2). It shows an area with many small farming villages, joined up by tracks. Which 3 places would become market towns?
(a) Make a careful copy of the map.
(b) Give each place an accessibility score by counting up how many tracks lead into it (some have already been done for you).
(c) The 3 places with highest scores will be the most accessible places – they would become the market towns. Mark them on your map with a larger circle.

4 What is the distance between the market towns on your map? Why do you think that market towns were often this distance apart?

5 Look carefully at the photo:
(a) What seems to be the main activity at the market?
(b) What else is going on?
(c) How have the people come to the market?

6 Imagine you were at the market shown in the photo:
Either – describe what you think would be the sights and sounds of the market,
or – write a story about something unusual that happens at the market that day.

7 Have you ever visited a street market? What sort of things are sold in street markets today?

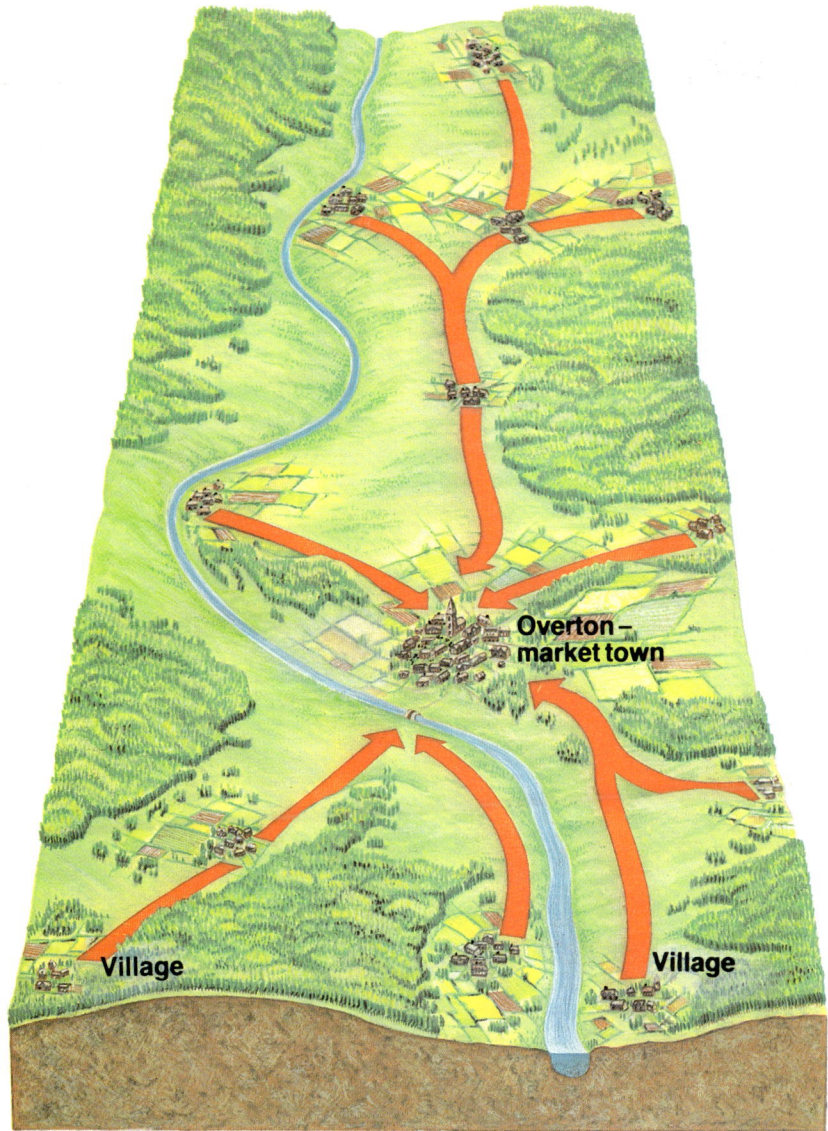

Figure 1

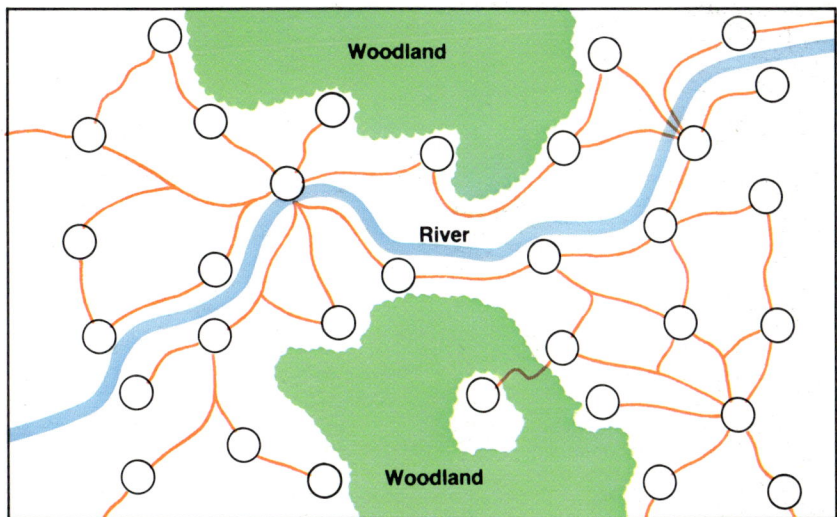

Figure 2

25

Industrial Revolution Cities

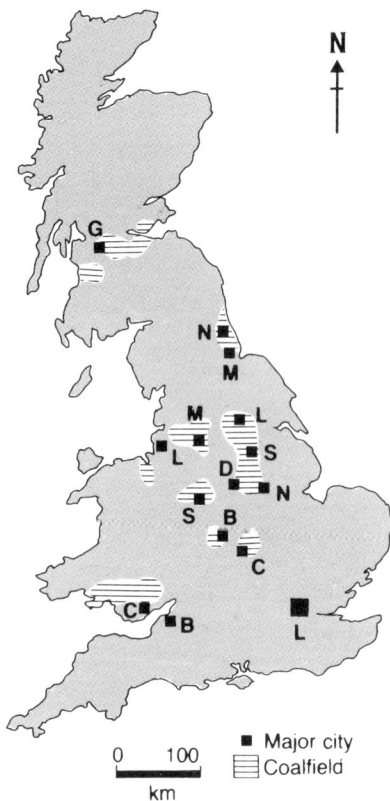

Figure 1

Birmingham is Britain's second largest city. It is a very important centre of industry. But as the line graph shows, Birmingham has not always been as important as it is today. Today 8 out of every 10 people in Britain live in towns and cities, but until the 1700s more people lived in villages than in towns. Until this time farming was still the most common way people earned their living. Then between about 1750 and 1850 there were great changes. This was the period we call the Industrial Revolution. Britain changed from being mainly an agricultural country to a modern industrial country, with most goods being produced by machines rather than by hand. With the growth of factories and industry, people moved from the countryside to the towns.

The steam engine was probably the most important invention of the Industrial Revolution, because it was steam engines that were used to power the new machines in the factories that were being built. Steam engines run on coal, and so many of the fastest growing towns of the Industrial Revolution were found on or close to Britain's **coalfields**. Birmingham was one, Manchester was another.

During the 1800s Britain was the world's most important industrial country. British industry imported raw materials from all over the world. In turn British goods were then exported all over the world. For this reason **ports**, such as Liverpool, grew into large industrial cities.

During the Industrial Revolution thousands of families moved into the industrial cities, looking for work in the new factories and coal mines. Somewhere had to be found for them to live. Rows of small terraced houses were built, usually close by the factories (see Fig. 3). Some of these terraces are still lived in today – like the one used as the set for 'Coronation Street'. But many of them have been demolished, and today people are moving away from these **inner city** areas to newer housing, often situated on the edge of cities. Many of the old factories too have closed, and this is another reason why people are moving away.

Figure 2: Liverpool Docks – the photograph was taken in 1964

1 Use Fig. 4 to work out the population of Birmingham at each of the dates shown on the line graph.

2 (a) In which 50 year period did Birmingham's population grow the fastest? (the steeper the line on the graph, the faster the growth of population).
(b) What has happened to Birmingham's population since 1951? Can you think of any reasons why this is happening?

3 Draw your own line graph to show the growth of Manchester's population since 1750.

1750	29,000
1800	72,000
1850	303,000
1900	607,000
1950	652,000
1980	535,000

4 Fig. 2 is a photograph of Liverpool. It shows the old port area, which was built during the Industrial Revolution (today there is a new port area, which is not shown in the photo).

Figure 3: These terraces in Salford, Lancashire, were built during the Industrial Revolution

Match each letter on the photo to one of these labels:
River Mersey
Docks
Warehouses
Dockside factory
Dry dock for ship repairs
Office block

5 Fig. 1 shows Britain's 15 largest cities.
(a) On your own blank map of Britain mark on the cities in their correct locations. Use your atlas to name each city – their first letters are shown.
(b) How many of the cities are ports on the coast?
(c) How many are on or very near coalfields?

6 **Project Idea:** The following people all had an important part to play in the Industrial Revolution. Try and find out more about them, and how they helped the Industrial Revolution:
Abraham Darby, James Watt, George Stephenson, James Brindley, Josiah Wedgwood.

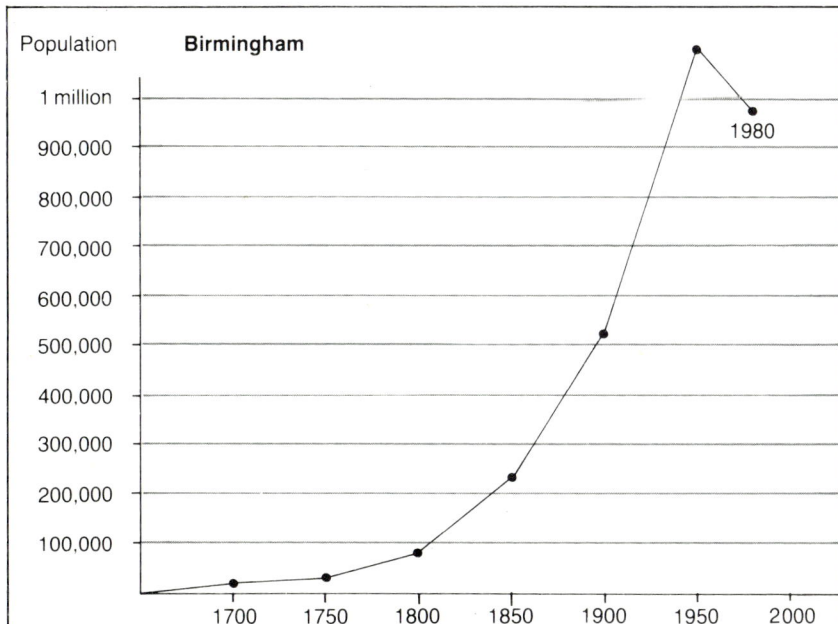

Figure 4

The Move from the Cities

The Industrial Revolution happened in Britain's towns and cities. It was in the cities that the new factories and offices were built, and so it was in the cities that the new jobs were to be found. The result was that thousands of people moved from the countryside to the towns and cities, which during the Industrial Revolution grew much larger.

Today the situation is very different. The population of most large towns and cities is no longer growing. The very largest cities are in fact getting smaller – people are moving away.

People are moving away mainly from the older parts of the cities – what are called the **inner city** areas. This is where houses, factories and warehouses were built in the earlier days of the Industrial Revolution. Today the inner city is no longer the best location for many businesses. The factory buildings are old, and not always suited to modern needs. Modern businesses want good road and motorway links, and these are found away from the congested inner city areas. As the businesses and jobs have declined in the inner cities, so has the number of people living there.

Even so, today the inner city areas have some of the worst unemployment problems in Britain. Much of the inner city housing is also old, and is being modernised and replaced.

Where do the people and businesses that leave the inner city go to? Some have moved to new housing or industrial estates on the edge of the city. Some have gone to other smaller towns and villages. Others have moved to one of the 33 new towns that governments have set up over the past 40 years.

Figure 1: This power station at Buildwas, Shropshire, was built on a greenfield site

The movement away has put a lot of pressure on some parts of the countryside. A large new housing or industrial development on a **greenfield site** must cause big changes in that area of countryside. Many country people do not like these changes. They feel that the character of their environment is being changed for the worse. Fig. 1 shows one example of an industrial development on a greenfield site.

The planners have a difficult job. A country like Britain is constantly changing, and so it is not possible to stop all new developments in the countryside. One of the planners' jobs is to try to make sure that new development happens in the most suitable places, and that the character of the countryside is not changed too much.

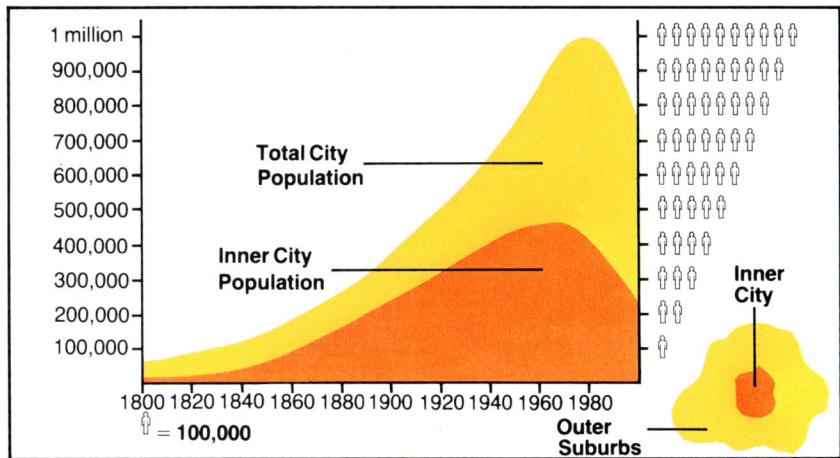

Figure 2

1 The graph (Fig. 2) shows how the population of a large British city has changed.
(a) When did the population of the city as a whole stop growing? What was the total population then?
(b) How many people does the city have now?
(c) Work out the population of the inner city area for each of the dates shown, and describe how the inner city population has changed.

2 Why are most of a city's older buildings concentrated in the inner city area?

3 What is the main reason why people are having to move from inner city areas?

4 Look at Figs. 3 and 4.
(a) Which plan shows the older, inner city housing?
(b) Compare the two plans, and describe as many differences as you can.

5 What is meant by a greenfield site for a new factory?

6 Look at the photo (Fig. 1). List all the ways that this area seems to have been affected by the development of new industry and housing.

7 What sort of people might object to the sort of development shown in Fig.1? Why do you think they might object?

8 What benefits might a power station, like the one in Fig. 1, bring to the local area?

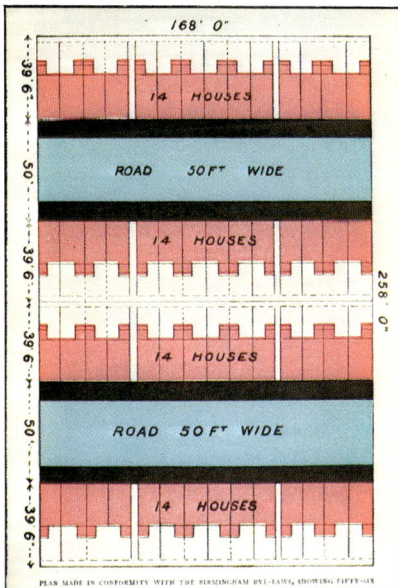

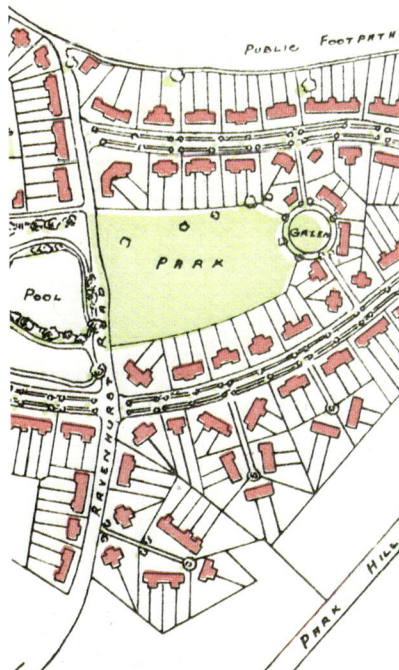

Figures 3 and 4

29

A Public Inquiry

Conbrick, a large construction company, would like to build a large estate of new houses in Overton.

What is Overton like?

Overton is a small market town, with a long history. Today it has a population of 12,000 people. In the town centre there are the sort of shops you would expect to find in any small town. At the edge of town there is a small new industrial estate. Many Overton people however work in a larger town 12 miles away. Overton has a sports centre, a secondary school, and three primary schools.

What do Conbrick want to build?

Conbrick's estate would have 300 houses. This would add about 1000 people to Overton's population. The estate would include a range of houses of different types and prices. Conbrick would also build 20 old peoples' flats, which it would then give to the local council. There are two possible sites where Conbrick could build their estate – they already own the land in both places.

Holding a public inquiry

Because a development as large as this could affect many people living in and around Overton, a **public inquiry** is to be held. A public inquiry is an open meeting, at which anybody from the local community can give their views on the proposed development.

Chamber of Commerce
You represent the people who own and run shops and businesses in Overton. Would more people be good or bad for business?

Residents of Underham
You live in the small village of Underham, a few miles from Overton. How would either estate affect you?

Overton Anti-traffic Group
For some years now you have been trying to reduce the amount of traffic in the centre of Overton. How would either estate affect traffic?

Residents of North Overton
You live in the area closest to the North Site. How would the estate, and more people and traffic affect you?

Conbrick Construction
You represent the company. Obviously you want to build an estate. The North Site would be cheaper for you, but either site would do.

Residents of Overton Manor
The manor is an historic manor house that has been divided into five flats. How would either estate affect you?

School Governors
You represent the four schools in Overton. A new estate would mean about 300 more children of all ages. How would this affect your schools?

Residents of South Overton
You live in the area closest to the South Site. How would the estate, and more people and traffic affect you?

---

1 You are going to hold the public inquiry. Each person in the class should join one of the groups outlined in the boxes. At the inquiry your job will be to give what you think would be the views of the group of people described in your box.

2 In your group, study the plans on page 31 carefully, and discuss what you think your views should be.
 – Are you in favour of an estate being built at all?
 – If so, which estate do you think would be better?
 Decide who will be your group's official spokesman at the inquiry.

3 At the inquiry:
 – First, each spokesman in turn gives his or her group's views.
 – Then anybody else has the right to speak – but remember, wait for the chairperson to ask you to speak, and only one person should speak at a time.
 – At the end of the inquiry there will be a vote to decide which, if any, of the developments should be allowed.

4 **After the inquiry:** Write down your views on the matter. Do you agree with what was decided at the inquiry? Explain your views as fully as you can.

5 **Project Idea:** Look through your local newspapers to see what public inquiries there have been in your area recently. Find out what the inquiries were for, and as many other details as you can.

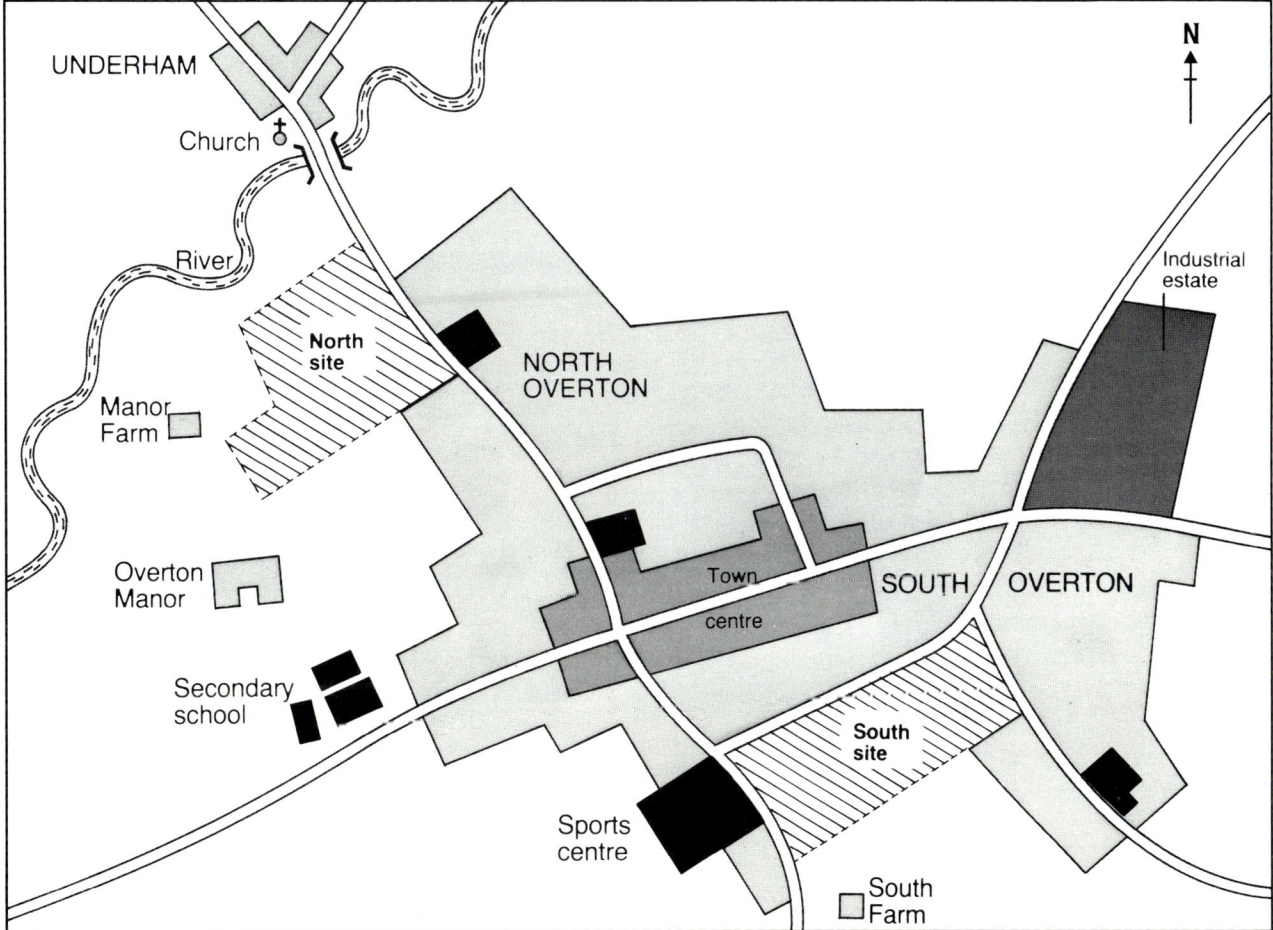

UNDERHAM

Church

River

Manor
Farm

North
site

NORTH
OVERTON

Overton
Manor

Town
centre

SOUTH   OVERTON

Industrial
estate

Secondary
school

South
site

Sports
centre

South
Farm

N

	Houses		Schools and sports centre
	Shops and businesses		Farmland
	Industrial estate		Main roads

0   ½   1

kilometre

Zones in Towns

Whether you live in a village, town or city, and whether it has a population of 10 people or 10 million, it will have one thing in common with all other settlements – it is a place where people live. People's homes take up more space than any other activity.

In a small village there may not be much more than a few houses, and probably a pub, perhaps a shop or a post office. In a town or city houses will only be one of many ways that the land is used. Towns have many different activities, and the larger the place the more activities it has. Fig. 1 shows the main activities you would find in a large town.

Where do a town's different activities take place? They are not all jumbled up. In which part of the town would you find most shops and offices? Are factories usually found mixed with houses, or with other factories? Any town or city has a number of different **zones**. Each zone is a part of the town where one type of activity is most important.

The busiest and most complicated zone is the town centre, as many different activities are found there. Most of them are businesses of some sort or other – for example shops, offices, banks, hotels, cinemas. For this reason the town centre is called the **Central Business District**, or **CBD** for short.

Not many people actually live in the CBD. Housing zones are found away from the town centre. Different types of housing are often found in different zones. The newest houses are found at the edge of town.

Factories, warehouses and other industrial activities form separate zones. Industry zones are often found close to important transport routes. In the past many factories were built by canals or railway lines – like those shown in the photo of Hebden Bridge (Fig. 4). Today factories and warehouses are often built close to main roads. Fig. 2 shows how a town might be divided up into different zones.

Figure 1

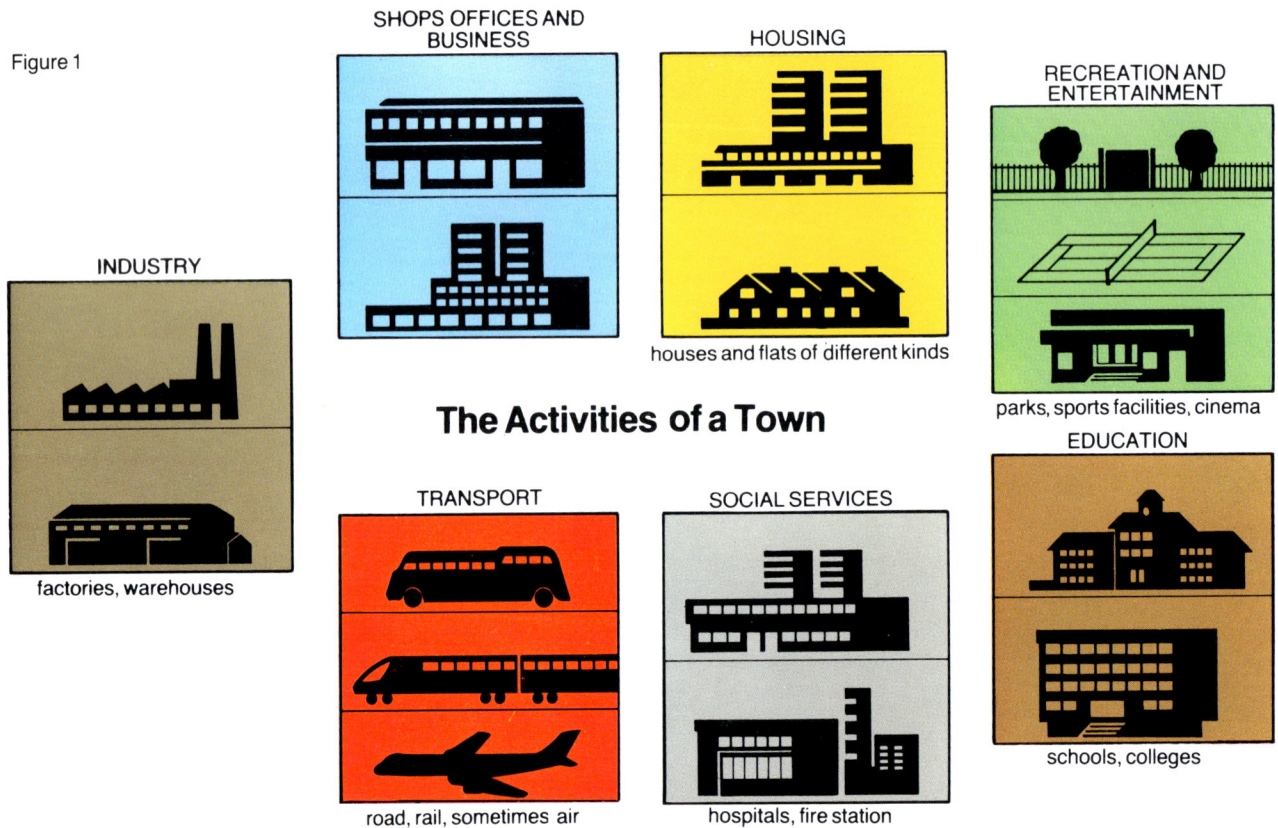

SHOPS OFFICES AND BUSINESS

HOUSING

houses and flats of different kinds

RECREATION AND ENTERTAINMENT

parks, sports facilities, cinema

INDUSTRY

factories, warehouses

The Activities of a Town

TRANSPORT

road, rail, sometimes air

SOCIAL SERVICES

hospitals, fire station

EDUCATION

schools, colleges

1 Using Fig. 1 make a list of the main activities of a town. From your local area think of an actual example of each activity.

2 (a) Here is a list of 20 different activities. Write them in a table like the one shown in Fig. 3.
post office, supermarket, hospital, international airport, bus station, theatre, newsagent, furniture shop, butcher, estate agent, public house, secondary school, indoor swimming pool, hotel, fire station, polytechnic, shoe shop, ice rink, church, travel agent
(b) For each activity say whether you think it would be found in the different sized places at the top of the table. The first two have been done for you.
(c) How many of the activities are found in each place?
(d) Explain what your table shows about the number and type of activities found in places of different sizes.

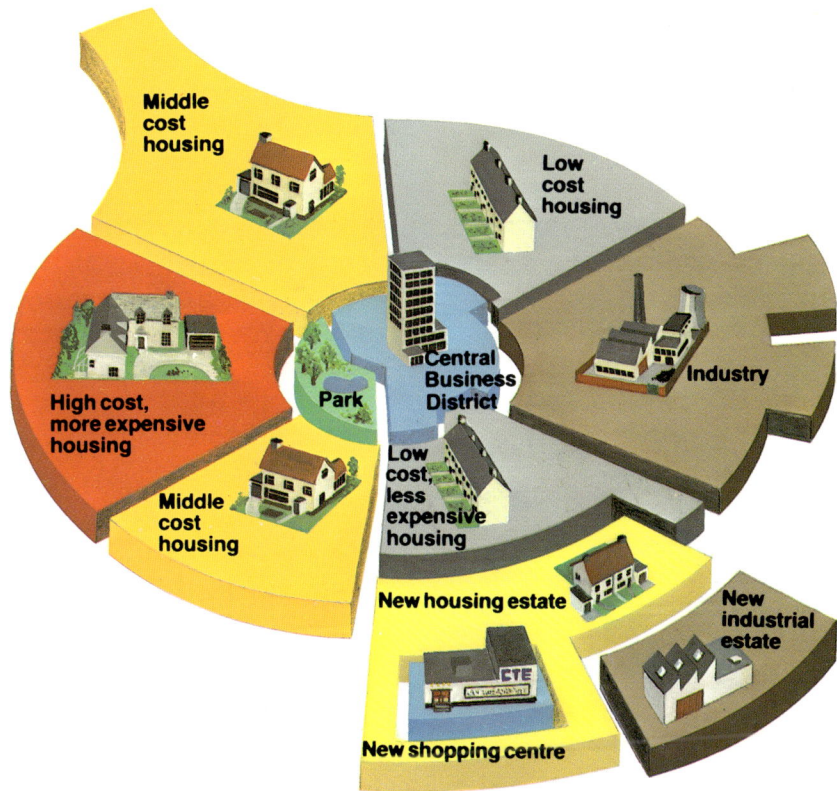

Figure 2

Activity	Village	Small Town	Large Town	Large City
Post Office	√	√	√	√
Supermarket	X	√	√	√

Figure 3

Figure 4: Hebden Bridge, Yorkshire. You can just see a canal between the blocks of flats and the older housing by the factory.

3 What do the initials CBD stand for? Why is this zone of a town given that name?

4 Why are industrial zones often found close to main transport routes?

5 Look at Fig. 4.
(a) What types of transport routes serve the factories shown?
(b) Is the housing all of the same age?
(c) Why do you think that houses were built as close as this to the factories?

33

Patterns of Work

There are hundreds of different sorts of jobs in Britain.

★ Some people work in offices, others work in factories, some people work outdoors, others work at home.
★ Some people have full-time jobs, working for 5 or more days a week. Others work part-time, or for only a part of the year. At any one time there will be others without a job, who are looking for work.
★ In some jobs people have to travel around a lot, in others they always work at the same place.

To live the sort of lives we do, we depend very much on other people to provide many of the things we want. How many things are there in your home which you or your family have made for yourselves? Take the example of a family car. You can only own a car after lots of other people have worked to make it. It takes the jobs of many more people to help you run the car.

Some jobs shown in Fig. 2 would be found in your local area. Others would take place in different parts of the country, or even in other countries of the world.

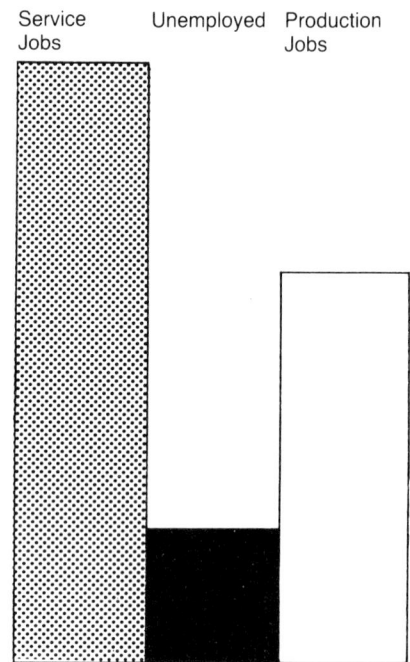

Figure 1 — Service Jobs, Unemployed, Production Jobs. Scale 1 cm = 2 million people, so 1 mm = 200,000 people

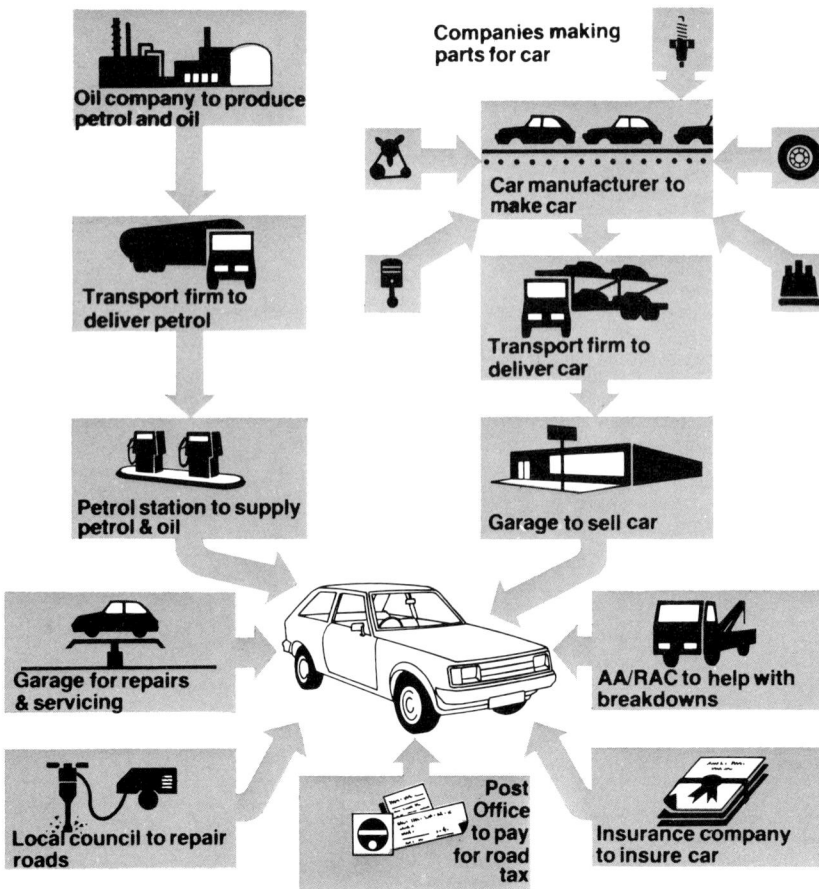

Oil company to produce petrol and oil

Transport firm to deliver petrol

Petrol station to supply petrol & oil

Garage for repairs & servicing

Local council to repair roads

Companies making parts for car

Car manufacturer to make car

Transport firm to deliver car

Garage to sell car

AA/RAC to help with breakdowns

Post Office to pay for road tax

Insurance company to insure car

Figure 2

Although they are all connected with your car, there is one very important difference between the jobs shown in Fig. 2. Some people's work involves them making or producing things. For example a person working in a car headlight factory has what we call a **production job**. On the other hand a person working at a petrol station does not actually produce anything. Their job involves selling things that somebody else has already produced. This is called a **service job**. The petrol station attendant provides car owners with a service, by selling them petrol and other products.

In Britain more people work in service jobs than in production jobs, as Fig. 1 shows.

1 In your own words explain the difference between a production job and a service job.

2 (a) Which of the jobs shown in the 3 photos are production jobs, and which service jobs?
(b) How many of these people have production jobs, and how many have service jobs?
steelworker, bank clerk, travel agent, teacher, farmer, garage mechanic, secretary, shipbuilder, shop assistant

3 Using the scale shown in Fig. 1, work out the number of people in each of the three groups.

4 Follow these instructions to make your own copy of Fig. 2:
– use one colour for production jobs
– use a second colour for service jobs
– use a third colour to put a thick margin around any of the jobs you would find in your local area

5 At the beginning of the opposite page different sorts of jobs are described. Write them down in a list, and try and give an example of each from your local area

6 In your local area there will be some locations where a lot of jobs are concentrated – an industrial estate, for example. Name these places, and say whether the people who work there have mainly production or service jobs, or a mixture of both.

7 The figures on the right show the work pattern in three different places. Use the figures to draw three divided bars – use a scale of 1 mm for each 1%.

An operator thinning glass

Coal miners

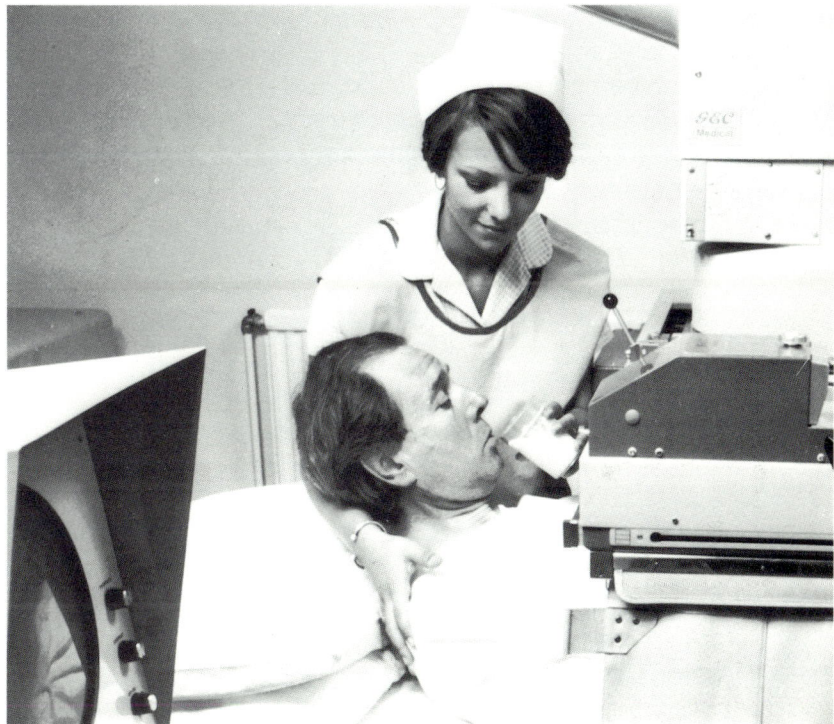
A nurse

	Production Jobs	Unemployed	Service Jobs
Place A	29%	27%	44%
Place B	18%	9%	73%
Place C	51%	15%	34%

8 Which of these three descriptions do you think fits each of the three divided bars you have drawn?
– market town with few factories
– town which has a large steelworks
– town where a large factory has recently closed

Shopping Around

In the past people had to produce for themselves most of the things that they needed. Today we buy most of the things we need in shops. This means that there are lots of different sorts of shops, selling an enormous variety of goods.

Because we rely on shops we have to travel to buy the things we need. For some goods we do not want to travel very far – to buy a newspaper, or a loaf of bread, or a bag of crisps, we want somewhere close by. These are what we could call **everyday goods**. We may not buy these things every single day, but they are the sort of everyday items that we shop for often.

But to buy say clothes or shoes we are usually more interested in being able to look around and choose. This means we want to go somewhere where there are a number of shops to give us a choice. We buy goods such as clothes and shoes less often – they are what we could call **occasional goods** – but we are prepared to travel further to buy them.

1 In your own words explain the difference between everyday goods and occasional goods.

2 Why are most people prepared to travel further to buy occasional goods?

3 How many of the shops listed below sell everyday goods, and how many sell mainly occasional goods?
chemist, electrical goods shop, department store, newsagent, greengrocer, ironmonger, jeweller, butcher, record shop, food supermarket

4 Look at the photo in Fig. 1:
(a) How many shop names can you make out? Make a list of them.
(b) What sort of things does each shop sell?
(c) How many of the shops sell occasional goods?
(d) Do you think the photo was taken in a village, small town, or large town? Give the reasons for your answer.

5 (a) From your local area name five examples of shops that sell everyday goods, and five that sell occasional goods.
(b) Where is the largest concentration of occasional shops in your local area?

6 What is the largest shop you remember being in? What was it and what sort of goods did it sell?

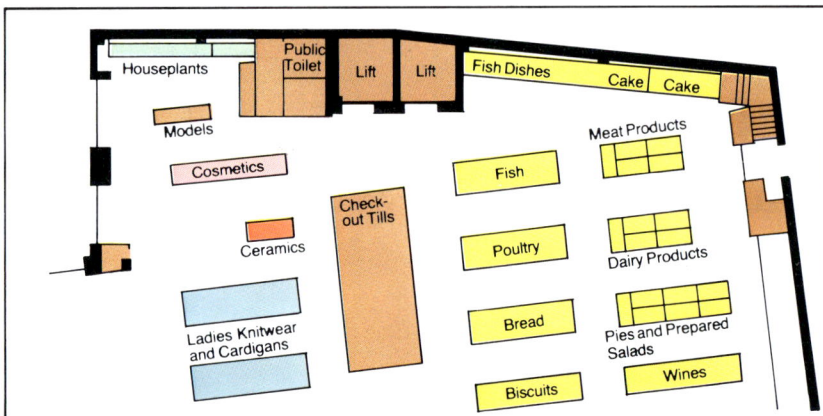

Above left: Figure 1, a row of shops in Middlesex

Left: A plan of part of a department store, which sells a wide range of goods

A town acts as a shopping centre, both for the town's inhabitants, and for the people who live in the surrounding area. The larger the town the more shops and services it has, and so the more people it attracts. Also the larger the town the larger the surrounding area from which it attracts people. The area from which a town or city attracts shoppers is called its **service area** – in other words, it is the area which is served by the town's shops and businesses.

The map (Fig. 2) shows the area around the market town of Thame in Oxfordshire. Thame is a shopping centre for the local area. A survey was carried out in Thame, and the figures in the box (Fig. 3) show where people came from to shop in the town.

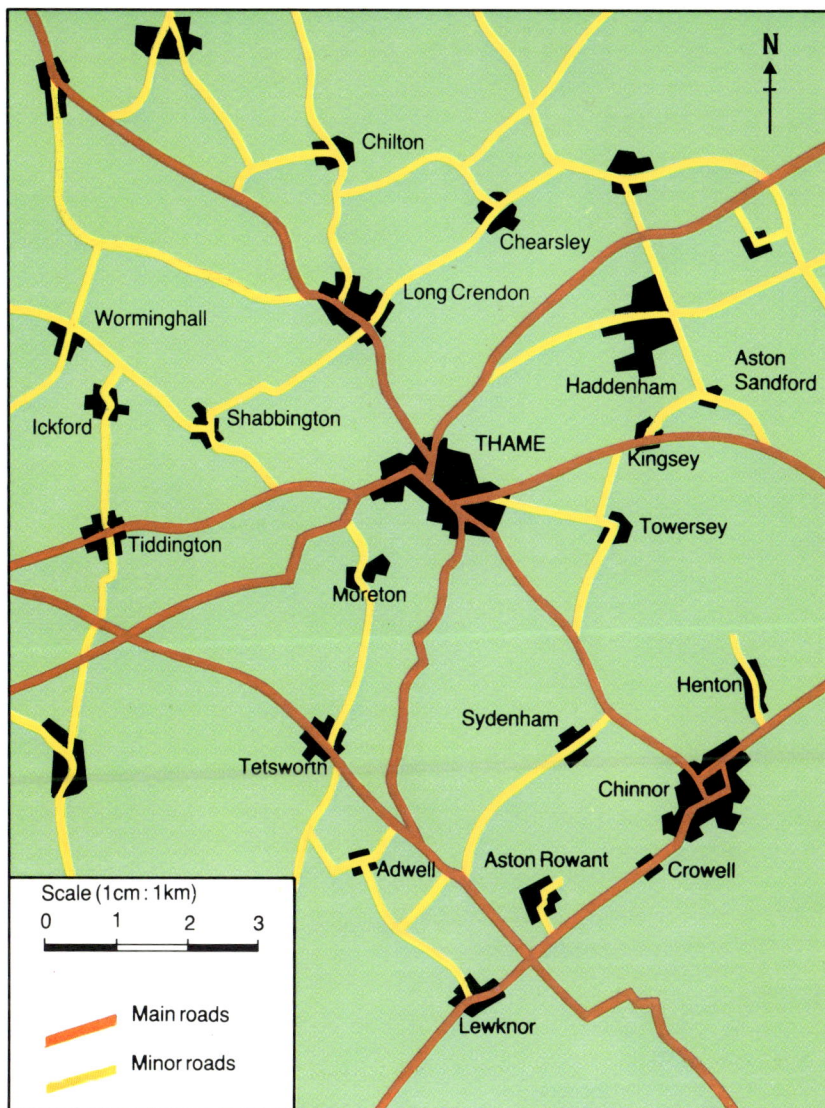

Figure 2

Where people came from to shop in Thame. Survey carried out on Tuesday October 19, 1982. (Thame residents have not been included.)

Chilton	1
Chearsley	2
Long Crendon	8
Shabbington	2
Ickford	2
Worminghall	1
Tiddington	2
Moreton	3
Tetsworth	2
Lewknor	1
Aston Rowant	2
Chinnor	9
Sydenham	2
Henton	2
Towersey	3
Kingsey	2
Haddenham	7

Figure 3

7 (a) Place a piece of tracing paper over the map, and on it mark all the places listed in the box.
(b) From each place draw a line for every person who went from that place to shop in Thame – so from Long Crendon you would draw 8 lines, to represent the shopping journeys of 8 people.

8 From the information on your map, draw a line around the edge of Thame's service area. Give your map the title 'The Service Area of Thame, Oxfordshire'.

9 What is the furthest distance people seem prepared to travel to Thame to shop?

10 Why do you think the survey showed only a few people going to Thame from some places, but more from others?

11 People living in the villages around Thame use other larger places for shopping, as well as Thame. Why is this?

Shopping Survey Ideas

Your Household Shopping

You can carry out the first part of this survey at home.

Aims: To find out
a Where different sorts of goods are bought
b How often different goods are bought

Method

1 Using a table, like the one in Fig. 1, make a list of 7 different everyday goods and 7 different occasional goods that people in your household have bought recently. (Fig. 1 gives you some ideas, but you may want to change some of the goods.)

2 By asking one or more people at home, fill in the other three columns in your table.

Results and conclusions

1 Draw up your results in two bar graphs – your teacher will show you how. Use one colour for everyday goods and another for occasional goods.

A mobile shopping van

What did your survey tell you? Use the information you found out to answer these questions:

2 Is it true that shopping for everyday goods is usually done closer to where you live? (If it is not true, are there any special reasons why not?)

3 Is it true that occasional goods are usually bought less often than everyday goods?

4 Are there certain places in your local area where either the everyday goods, or the occasional goods, are most often bought?

5 What is the average distance travelled to buy the everyday goods? To work this out, add up all the distances for everyday goods, and divide the total by seven (or by however many different goods you had in your survey).

6 What is the average distance travelled to buy occasional goods? How does it compare with the everyday goods average?

7 Was the pattern of shopping in your household as you expected? Explain your answer as fully as you can.

Type of Goods	Where would this usually be bought?	How far away is that?			About how often is it bought?				
		Less than 1 km	1-5 km	Over 5 km	More than once a week	Once a week	Once a fortnight	Once a month	Occasionally
Everyday Goods									
1. Bread									
2. Newspaper/Magazines									
3. Canned goods – such as baked beans									
4. Fresh vegetables									
5. Soap									
6. Frozen foods – such as beefburgers									
7. Eggs									
Occasional Goods									
1. Shoes									
2. Any item of furniture									
3. Blouse/Shirt									
4. Any item of kitchen equipment									
5. Record									
6. Any item of electrical equipment									
7. Any item for the car									

Figure 1

A Shopping Centre Survey

This survey can be carried out at any place where there is a concentration of shops in your local area.

Aims: To find out
a What sort of shops the centre has
b From where people travel to use the shops

What sort of shops?
Method
Use a table, like Fig. 2, to record the different types of shops. If you are not sure how to record any shops, note their names and what they sell.

Type of Shops Survey Place	
Everyday Goods Shops	
Food Shops	√ √ √
Non-food shops	√
Occasional Goods Shops	
Clothes	√ √
Shoes	√
Electrical goods	√
(Think about how many other types of shops you want to list)	

Figure 2

Figure 3: Carrying out a shopping centre survey and (below) a shopping questionnaire

Shopping Questionnaire	Place		Date		Time		
'Good morning/afternoon, we are from ____ school, and we are carrying out a shopping survey. Could you help us by answering a few questions? Thank you.'							
Q1 Where do you live?	Q2 About how far away is that?			Q3 About how often do you come to shop here?			
	Less than 1 km	1-5 km	More than 5 km	More than once a week	Once a week	Once a fortnight	Once a month	Occas-ionally
[Fill in each person's information on a separate line]								

Results and conclusions
1 Draw up your results in a bar graph.

2 Does the centre have mainly everyday or occasional goods shops?

How far do people come to shop there?
Method
To find this out you will need to fill in a **questionnaire,** like the one shown in Fig. 3. It is best to stand outside a shop – and remember, you must be polite! You should tell people where you are from, and what you are doing. If they don't want to answer your questions, that is their right – but thank them all the same!

Results and conclusions
1 If you have carried out the survey as a class group, start by combining your questionnaire results.

2 On a bar graph show the results from your questionnaire which show how often people use the shopping centre.

3 If you can, use a local map to plot where people have come from to shop at the centre.

4 Does the map show the service area of the shopping centre you surveyed? Try and mark it on your map.

5 From how far away did people come to shop there?

6 Do you think the centre is used mainly for everyday or for occasional shopping?

7 Is the centre used mainly by people who live close by, or does it serve a wider area?

Changes – Traffic in Towns

Have you ever talked to your grandparents, or an elderly neighbour, about what life was like when they were young? I expect they would say it was very different. For one thing the pace of life was slower, especially in the towns and cities. There seems to be more noise and bustle in towns today, and one of the main reasons is that there are more cars and motor vehicles.

People want cars, because a car gives them the freedom to go where they want, when they want. Yet sometimes it seems as if cars will bring towns to a grinding halt. You must have experienced the frustration of being trapped in a traffic jam. The worst **traffic congestion** is often in and around the main shopping centres, because that is where most people want to go.

Towns have had to change to cope with more cars. New roads have been built and old ones widened. But there is a limit to what town planners can do, without pulling the whole place down and starting again, which nobody wants. If you cannot redesign towns to cope with cars, you have to persuade people to use their cars less. Almost all towns now charge for car parking, and there is strict control over where people can park their cars. Some towns have special bus lanes, and as only buses can use them, they do not get caught in traffic jams. The result is a quicker and more reliable bus service. Another scheme is to close some streets to traffic, and make them for **pedestrian** use only – people have rights too!

Figure 1: London Street, Norwich, Norfolk, in (left) 1883; (below left) 1968; (below) 1983

1 Are there any places in your local area where traffic jams regularly occur? Explain why you think they happen there.

2 Is traffic congestion in towns more serious at any particular times of the day do you think? Explain why.

3 (a) For a shopping centre you know, say how car parking is controlled.
(b) What other ways are used to control where cars can and cannot go?

4 Look at Fig. 1: What are the possible advantages and disadvantages of a pedestrian only shopping street for (a) shoppers, and (b) shopkeepers?

5 How can providing a better bus service help towns with their traffic problems?

6 Despite expensive parking and improved bus services, some people prefer to drive right into the town centre. Why do you think this is?

7 In recent years British Rail has run a press and TV campaign which encourages people to leave their cars at home and travel by train instead. Design a poster which encourages people to travel by bus rather than by car.

8 **Project idea:** Do an interview with an elderly person you know. Ask them what they think have been the greatest changes in their local area over the last 50 years. Either record your interview on tape, or write a report of the interview afterwards.

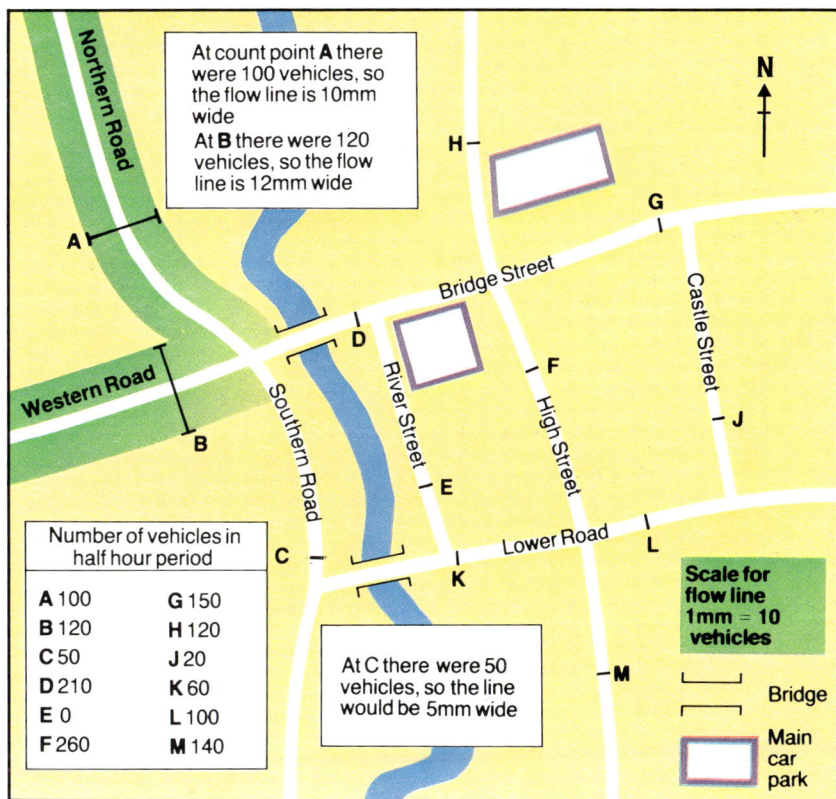

At count point **A** there were 100 vehicles, so the flow line is 10mm wide
At **B** there were 120 vehicles, so the flow line is 12mm wide

Number of vehicles in half hour period	
A 100	G 150
B 120	H 120
C 50	J 20
D 210	K 60
E 0	L 100
F 260	M 140

At C there were 50 vehicles, so the line would be 5mm wide

Scale for flow line
1mm = 10 vehicles

Bridge

Main car park

Figure 2

A Traffic Survey

How many cars, lorries and buses use this road? Is this road busier than that one? Where are the likely traffic congestion points? These are the sort of questions that can be answered by carrying out a traffic survey.

The map (Fig. 2) shows the road plan of a town centre. At each of the points marked by a letter, a traffic count was taken. The figures in the box show how many vehicles passed each point during a half hour period.

1 Use a copy of the map, and the traffic count figures to make a flow diagram. The more traffic there is, the wider the road is drawn on a flow diagram. Part of the flow diagram has been done for you – take care to use the same scale.

2 Using your flow diagram answer these questions:
(a) Which is the busiest road?
(b) Which 3 points in the town are most likely to suffer from traffic jams do you think?
(c) Which street is for pedestrians only?
(d) Which street do you think is for buses only?
(e) On which roads might it be a good idea to make special bus lanes?

3 Are there any ways that you think the traffic flow in this town could be improved? Write a report giving your views and ideas.

Changes – Shopping Patterns

More people than ever before now own a car. Because of this the way people do their shopping is changing. Instead of buying food every day, they can use their cars to do one large shop which will last the week. This means using a shop which has plenty of car parking close by. In crowded town centres there is little room for shops to have their own car parks. Where is there enough room? At the edge of town.

In the last few years many large **hypermarkets**, or superstores, have been built. These are very large shops that sell food, as well as a whole range of other household goods (Fig. 1). The advantage they offer customers is plenty of free car parking, close enough for people to be able to just load up their cars and drive away (Fig.2)

Not everyone welcomes the new hypermarkets. Some city centre shops are worried that they will lose business, if their customers decide to use the edge-of-town shopping centres instead. Their answer is to press city authorities to improve city centre car parking, by building multi-storey car parks, for example. Their view is that if people can park more easily they will still use the city centre,

because there is a wider range of shops, and therefore more choice. Nor does everybody have a car. Without your own transport it is not easy to make use of a hypermarket. Whether or not to allow the development of edge-of-town shopping centres can be a difficult question for city authorities, as many different people might be affected.

A hypermarket for Standbury?
Standbury is a city of 120,000 people. Loprice Ltd want to build a large hypermarket at the edge of the city. The site they have chosen is shown in Fig. 4. Some local people are in favour of the hypermarket, but others are against it.

1 Look at Figs. 1 and 2: say in what ways a hypermarket is different from a large supermarket in a town centre.

2 Why do you think that Loprice chose that site in Standbury?

3 Six different groups of people are described in the box (Fig. 3). What views do you think each group would have on the proposed hypermarket? Would they be in favour, or against it? Explain your answer fully.

4 Do you think that Standbury City Council should or should not allow Loprice to build the hypermarket? Give the reasons for your decision.

Figure 1: The interior of a hypermarket in Caerphilly, Glamorgan

Figure 2: A hypermarket in Newport, Gwent

Shopkeepers in the city centre of Standbury

Shopkeepers in Upper Easterley and Lower Easterley

People who live in the Easterley district of Standbury

People who live in other parts of Standbury

People who live in the countryside outside Standbury

People who live in Standbury who do not have the use of a car

Figure 3

Shopping centres | Motorway | Norton Easterley Westerham | districts of Standbury | 0 1 km

Built-up area | Main roads

Figure 4

Shopping and computers

Computers are changing the way shops are run, and soon may change the way we do our shopping.

Big stores already use computers to do their accounts and to help keep a check on their stocks of goods. Some shops now use tills that are directly linked to a computer. Instead of reading the price and ringing it up, the checkout operator simply passes what looks like a pencil over the **bar code** on each product being bought.

The bar code is a pattern of 28 lines of different thicknesses that is now found on the packaging of many grocery and other products. You can see one on the back cover of this book. Each different product has a slightly different bar code. The thing that looks like a pencil is in fact a low power laser

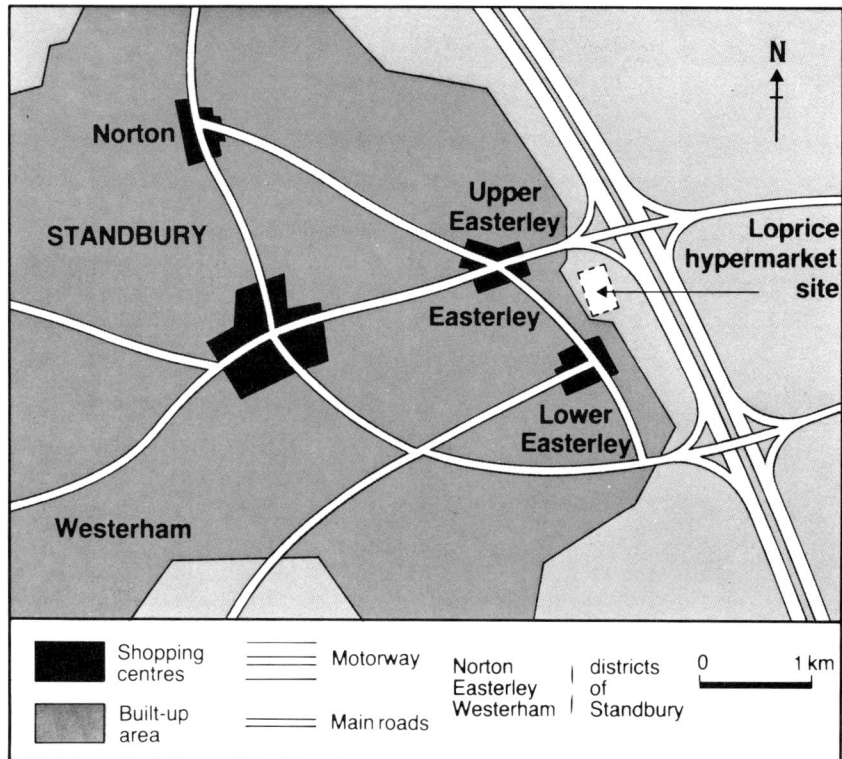

beam. The laser 'reads' the bar code. The till unit is linked to a computer that holds the prices of all the shop's products. As soon as the laser beam passes over the bar code the computer identifies the product, and displays its name and price on the till screen. The computer also adds up the final bill, and prints a receipt for the customer. At the same time the computer is also keeping an up-to-date record of the stocks of different products in the shop.

Before long many people could be using computers to do their shopping without even going to the shop. If you have a computer terminal in your home, connected to the shop's computer, you can simply key in your order. At the shop the computer prints out your order, and someone collects together the goods, and arranges for them to be delivered.

1 (a) Explain how the bar code computerised system operates.
(b) How does this help the shop save money?

2 In the future, if you used your home computer to order goods for delivery, they would probably be more expensive than if you yourself went to the shop to buy them. Explain why you think this would be so.

3 In the future a computer in your home could do much more than just order your shopping. Imagine that you lived in a fully computerised house. Write an account of a typical day at home – how would you use the computer, and what tasks could it do for you?

43

Environments of the Future – the Countryside

What is your mental picture of typical countryside? Green fields and woods, grazing farm animals and peace and quiet?

If you live in a large city you may have little contact with the countryside – your view of it may be from a car on the motorway, or from your seat on the train. But if you lived on a modern farm your picture of the countryside might be very different.

Over the last 100 years farming has changed a lot. It has become a much more scientific business. Chemical fertilizers and pesticides are sprayed on fields, scientifically developed seeds are used, while complicated and expensive machines carry out many of the day-to-day tasks on the farm.

More and more animals are kept in specially designed buildings for most or all of the year. Keeping animals indoors means that a farmer is not so dependent on the weather. In future will more animals be kept and crops produced indoors? It is already possible to grow plants without soil (as Fig. 1 shows) – the roots float in water that has carefully measured amounts of plant foods added to it. All these changes have come about because all the time farmers are trying to

Figure 1

produce more from their land. Fig. 2 shows one prediction, made in 1900, of what farming might be like in the year 2000. Some of the ideas look a little old-fashioned but others, such as the computer-controlled automatic harvesting system, may well be in use by 2000.

As methods of farming, and transport, have changed, so has the look of the countryside. What will a typical area of countryside look like in another 100 years? Nobody really knows, but Fig. 3 is one possible picture of the countryside of the future.

1 Describe what a farm factory of the future might be like.

2 What different ways are there of transporting goods and people?

3 What are the three ways people are using artificial climates?

4 What is the oldest feature? What is it used for?

5 What ways of making heat and power are there?

6 Do you think it will be important to have nature reserves, or could the land be used in a better way?

7 Imagine that you were living in this sort of environment. What are the things about it that you would like or dislike? Explain your reasons as fully as you can.

Figure 2

EN L'AN 2000.

Figure 3

8 Imagine that you are standing in the farm factory area – make a large drawing of what you see around you.

9 Fig. 3 shows only one view of what the countryside might be like in the future. What do you think it might be like? Describe your ideas, and illustrate them with a drawing.

A Farm factory	**D** Computerised factory – more of the factory is underground
1 Artificial climate domes	
2 Reservoir tank	**E** Leisure centre
3 Multi-storey greenhouse	1 Traditional village holiday centre
4 Farm produce processing factory	2 Lakeside holiday chalets
5 Farm village	3 Sports dome with artificial climate
6 Balloon transport point	4 Solar heating panels
	5 Holiday caravan park
B Transport corridor	
1 Car transport tunnel – cars moved on conveyor belt	**F** Fish breeding farm
2 Vacuum pipeline for moving smaller goods	**G** Dehumanised zone – nature reserve
3 High speed monorail for moving heavier goods	**H** Timber zone
	J Farming Zone
C Windmill farm – for generating electricity	**K** Algae farm – algae grown for fertiliser and animal feed

Environments of the Future – Cities

The pace of change is increasing all the time, and nowhere are things changing faster than in the cities. In many parts of the world cities are growing more rapidly than ever before. Growth brings change. The cities have to change to cope with more people, and more of all the things the people want and need.

More people need more room – so the cities grow outwards, swallowing up the surrounding countryside. Or else they grow upwards – towers of glass and concrete to provide the space people need to live and work. 100 years ago there were no cars, no aeroplanes, no skyscrapers, no computers and fewer people. What will the cities be like in another 100 years? Will they continue to grow ever outwards and upwards? Or will they develop downwards, under the ground?

This monorail runs between Haneda Airport and the centre of Tokyo in Japan

We, as people, wouldn't like to live and work underground, never seeing the sun or breathing fresh air. But in 100 years time much of the work in factories and offices will be done by computers or computer-controlled robots. Will the factories of the future be below our feet?

The world's supplies of oil will have run out well before the next 100 years have passed. What will replace the petrol-driven car? Even today our cities are becoming clogged with traffic – can the cities afford to allow a new type of car to take over from the petrol-powered ones? Or will transport in the cities of the future be better organised? Movement of goods could either be underground or through the air – why clog the streets with lorries? Moving walkways could take people on short journeys. For longer journeys a computer-controlled 'personal movement bubble' could whizz you through the transport tubes to your destination anywhere in the city.

The populations of the largest cities in Britain are no longer growing. Yet the cities will still have to change. Much of the change will come in the older inner-city areas. In the 1960s and early 1970s many older inner-city houses were pulled down, and replaced by high-rise tower blocks. But most people did not like the towers as they were not good places to live in. Unlike the old terraced streets they had little sense of community – good views

In the future more city centres may look like Dallas, Texas

Figure 1

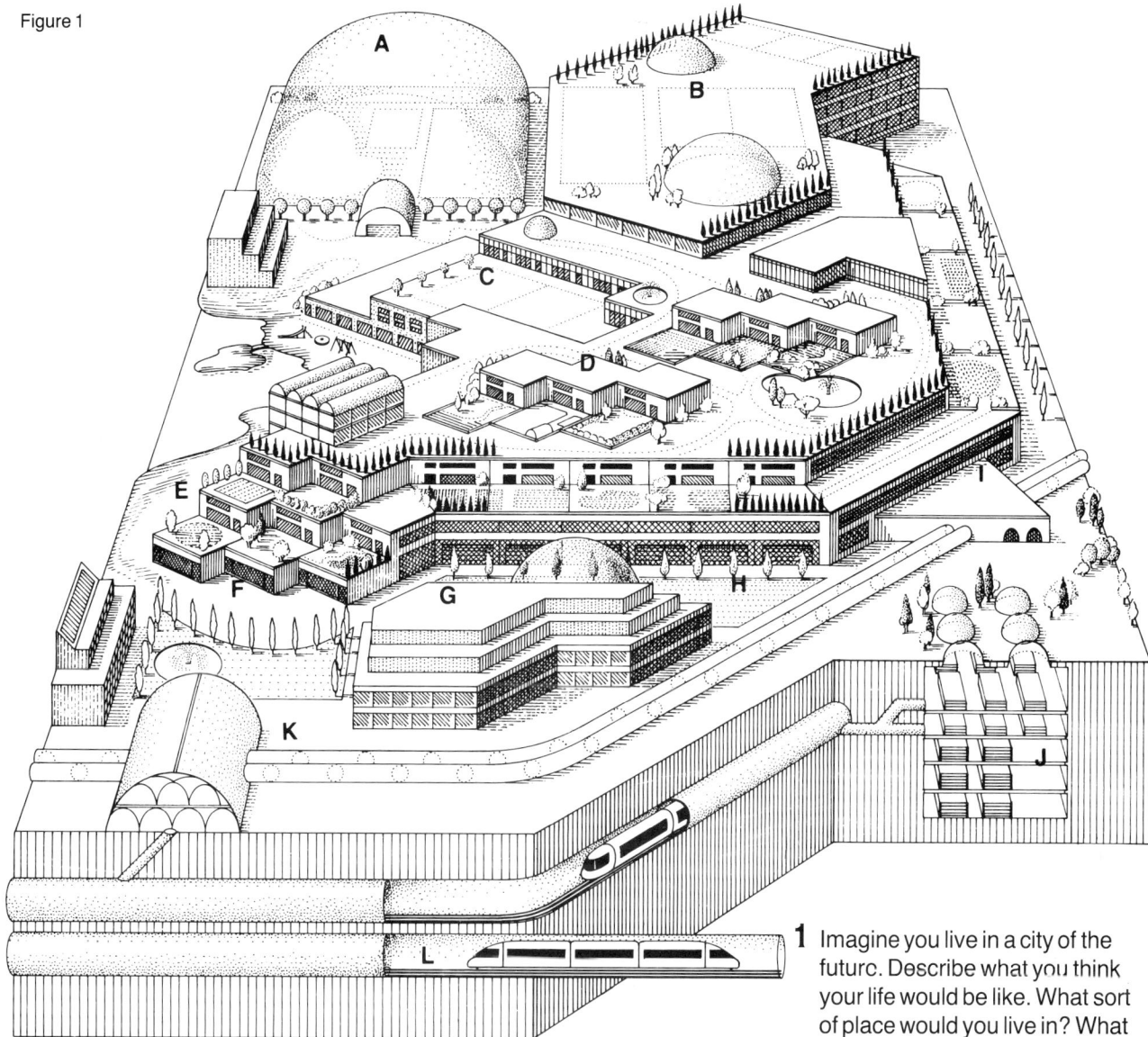

and a modern bathroom did not make up for the loss of a sense of belonging to a community. Between the towers there was plenty of open space. But too often this became a wasteland. For all the extra space nobody actually had their own little bit of garden to look after, somewhere to sit quietly or where the children could play safely.

Fig. 1 is just one view of what cities might look like in about 100 years time. What do you think?

A All weather leisure dome
B Sports facilities
C Flats for single people
D Family houses
E Old peoples' flats
F Shops
G Community centre
H Community courtyard
I City station
J Underground factory
K Personal movement bubbles within transport tubes
L Underground goods monorail

1 Imagine you live in a city of the future. Describe what you think your life would be like. What sort of place would you live in? What would you do? What would you eat and drink? What would you wear? Do some drawings to help you explain your ideas.

2 How do you think city transport will be organised in the future? Describe your ideas as fully as you can.

3 In what ways are the housing complexes shown in Fig. 1 different from the high-rise tower blocks built in Britain in the 1960s?

4 What do you think 'school' will be like in 100 years time?

Glossary

Act of Parliament: A law that has been passed by the British parliament.

Accessible: A place that is easily accessible is easy to get to.

Artificial: Used to describe anything that is made by people and is therefore not **natural.**

Bar code: A pattern of 28 lines of varying widths, printed on the packaging of shop goods, and used for computer identification of different goods.

Building style: The shape and appearance of a building.

Central Business District or **CBD:** The place in a town or city where there is the greatest concentration of shops, offices and businesses; often called the town centre.

Coalfield: A region which has large deposits of coal.

Community: All the people who live in a particular local area are members of its community.

Environment: Your surroundings at any one time, for example where you live or work; any environment is made up of both **natural** and **artificial** things.

Everyday goods: The sort of goods that people buy regularly and often, such as bread, milk and vegetables.

Exports: Goods or services made in one country which are then sold to a foreign country or countries.

Green Belt: An area of countryside around a town or city where development is strictly controlled.

Greenfield site: A situation when any buildings are constructed on land previously used for farming.

Grid reference: The method used to find an exact location on a map; a grid reference will either be a four figure or six figure reference.

Hypermarket: A large self-service store selling foods and other household items; it has plenty of space for customers' cars, and is usually located on the outskirts of a town.

Imports: Services or goods made in a foreign country but which are brought into your own country.

Industrial estate: An area in a town where there is a concentration of factories and warehouses.

Inner city: The area around the city centre which often contains much of the city's older housing and industrial areas.

Map: A diagram representing part or all of the Earth's surface. It can also show such features as roads, buildings, rivers, population distribution, weather, etc.

Map grid: The pattern of equal sized squares on a map that is used to give grid references.

Market: When people meet together in a certain place to buy and sell food and other goods.

Market town: A town in a rural area where there has been a regular market used by people from all over the surrounding area.

Natural: Used to describe anything that occurs in or is produced by nature, in other words not **artificially** made.

Occasional goods: The sort of goods, such as clothes or electrical items, that people only buy occasionally.

Pedestrian: Somebody who travels on foot.

Plan: A drawing to scale which shows the layout of a building.

Port: A place on the coast or a river where goods or people are loaded or unloaded from land transport to water transport, and vice versa.

Planning Permission: The permission that has to be given by a local council before any new building can be put up, or the use of a building changed.

Production job: Any job that is involved with making, or manufacturing anything.

Public enquiry: Held by the government or local council to look into a new development which will affect the local area; any member of the public can attend and give her or his views.

Questionnaire: A set of questions put to a number of people in order to gather certain information.

Scale: Used to turn distances on a map into actual distances on the ground; a map can have either a linear scale, or a statement of scale.

Service: Any activity which involves one or more people helping or assisting other people, for example a shop, bank or school.

Service area: The service area of a town is the area from which people travel to use the services provided by the town; the larger the town, the larger will be its service area. Also the term for the place on a motorway where people stop for petrol and food.

Service job: Any job that involves providing some sort of service to other people; a service job does not involve actually making anything.

Site: The actual piece of ground on which a building or settlement is positioned.

Traffic congestion: Where a road system cannot cope with the amount of traffic using it, thus resulting in a traffic jam.

Zone: An area or region which can be identified by a special feature; a town zone is an area of the town where one particular activity, such as housing or industry, is dominant.